Waterfalls
of Michigan

A Guide to More Than 130 Waterfalls in the Great Lakes State

Greg Kretovic

Adventure Publications
Cambridge, Minnesota

Dedication

To my family: Leah, Miles, Nora and Grant.

Disclaimer This book is meant as an introduction to the waterfalls of Michigan. It does not guarantee your safety in any way—when visiting waterfalls, you do so at your own risk. Neither Adventure Publications nor Greg Kretovic is liable for property loss or damage or personal injury that may result from visiting waterfalls. Before you visit a waterfall, be sure you have permission to visit the location, and always avoid potentially dangerous situations or areas, such as cliffs or areas with moving/deep water or areas where wildlife (snakes, insects) may be a concern. In particular, beware of slippery rocks, drop-offs, fast-moving or high water levels, and wilderness conditions. Your safety is your personal responsibility.

Cover photo by Greg Kretovic
Edited by Brett Ortler
Cover and book design by Lora Westberg

All photos by Greg Kretovic except author photo by Leah Kretovic (pg. 232)

10 9 8 7 6 5 4 3

Waterfalls of Michigan: A Guide to More Than 130 Waterfalls in the Great Lakes State
Copyright © 2018 by Greg Kretovic
Published by Adventure Publications
An imprint of AdventureKEEN
310 Garfield Street South
Cambridge, Minnesota 55008
(800) 678-7006
www.adventurepublications.net
All rights reserved
Printed in China
ISBN 978-1-59193-771-5 (pbk.); ISBN 978-1-59193-772-2 (ebook)

Acknowledgments

There were many people who helped me in my journey of visiting, photo-graphing and writing about Michigan's waterfalls. First and foremost, I have to thank my wife, Leah. This was a truly a team effort. Whether it was managing the household while I was gone nearly every weekend in the summers, or sitting in the van with the kids while I was out documenting a nearby waterfall, she never complained. She also played a big role in my writing and helping me stay calm while I worried about the looming deadline. Thank you for everything. I love you.

To my children, Miles, Nora and Grant. Thank you for putting up with me gone a lot and enduring some adventures to see waterfalls. They did some incredible hikes for only being 7, 5 and 2 years old at the time. I hope you cherish the memories we made.

To my extended family and friends, thank you for your support and encour-agement during the journey and the willingness to spread the word about this book. It is much appreciated. Thank you also to Charley MacIntosh and John Schwab for trusting me with your equipment that helped make this book possible. I can tell you it went to some incredible places! (Charley, I hope you're still enjoying your new laser rangefinder after I dropped your old one in the river at Big Pup Falls.) Thank you also to Gary and Wendy Gouin for opening your home to me while I was over in the Porkies area. Your open invitation and accommodations were greatly appreciated.

Thank you to Brett at Adventure Publications for assisting me along the way. With my many emails and phone calls, you were always very helpful and a great resource.

And finally, thank you to the wolf near Judson Falls and the bears at O Kun de Kun Falls and Big Falls for only leaving pawprints. You definitely added excitement to an already great adventure!

Table of Contents

Introduction

I moved to the Upper Peninsula (U.P.) of Michigan, to the city of Marquette, in the fall of 1998 after transferring to Northern Michigan University. I instantly fell in love with the area, the surrounding natural beauty and the seasons. With an Art & Design background, I was naturally drawn to photographing nature, including Lake Superior. Over the years, I traveled to many destinations around the U.P. capturing the amazing landscapes throughout the seasons. Waterfalls were always a favorite destination. I typically went for the popular ones or ones close to home because I didn't usually have the time to trek too long.

Then in the early spring of 2016, I was contacted by Adventure Publications and asked to do a book on Michigan Waterfalls. At this point, I had a decent collection of photographed U.P. waterfalls but little did I know how many more were out there and the amount of time and travel to see and document them. After consulting with Leah, my wife, we decided to go for it. This was going to be a team effort.

For nearly a year and a half, I did nothing but live and breathe waterfalls. Since they're hard to photograph in the winter (and we have long winters),

Greg Kretovic and family

I was under a time crunch to reach them with a short viewing season. Every weekend (late spring through fall) I was typically plotting which part of the U.P. I would visit, how many I could actually visit within a trip and whether I was going to camp or make the drive home in a day. It was very challenging and there were a few roadblocks along the way.

In the end, what I learned is the U.P. has some really, really incredible places off the beaten path; and, to me, the best waterfalls aren't the ones advertised on billboards. I will admit, some of the waterfalls are very challenging to reach with long hikes and steep descents but you are well rewarded for your efforts. What I also loved is that the journey to the waterfalls will take you to some incredible other areas that you may have not likely visited. They include great drives along Lake Superior, hiking to awesome vistas, visits to old copper mines and some really neat, small U.P. towns with kind, genuine people.

I hope you enjoy the treks to the waterfalls within this guide and are able to create lasting memories like I have.

Michigan Waterfalls

The waterfalls in Michigan come in a variety of shapes and sizes—from long gradual cascades to sheer, plunging drops into Lake Superior. Michigan is also unique; even though the state is separated into two peninsulas, there's only one official waterfall in the Lower Peninsula. So, in this guide you'll be exploring the many parts of the Upper Peninsula—also referred to as God's Country. Some of the waterfalls are convenient and visible from the road while others require determination and adventure. There truly is a waterfall for everyone to see.

Seasonal Variations

Waterfalls, like everything in nature, change throughout the seasons. Michigan's four distinct seasons can play a big part in how a waterfall will look. During a hot, dry summer you may find some waterfalls flowing down to a trickle and in the dead of winter they are completely frozen.

In the descriptions, I note the best times to visit certain waterfalls and I tried to reference the time of year when I was there. And while most waterfalls aren't that popular or accessible in winter, a few waterfalls are definitely worth a trek in winter, so I've noted those as well.

Trespassing/Private Land Info

At the time of this writing, the waterfalls in this book are located on federal, state, and private land, but all are open to the public. Wherever a waterfall is located, please respect the land and practice leave-no-trace ethics. If visitors litter or are otherwise irresponsible, land managers or property owners may close off access to these beautiful treasures. Also, please keep in mind that over time, property ownership can change (or landowners can change their mind about opening up their land to visitors) so please respect any signage denying access.

Safety Info

As you may have guessed, visiting a waterfall includes an element of danger. Flowing water, slick rocks and sharp elevation changes all pose a hazard, and once you get closer to a waterfall, mud, moss, and ice can all create a very slick and precarious situation. At some waterfalls in this book, there are barriers, fencing and even signage to help persuade you to stay away from the dangerous areas. Please respect these barriers, which are often there for a reason, such as previous injuries or fatalities at the falls in question.

At other falls, there are no barriers. As always, please respect nature because it can take only one misstep to put yourself in real danger. Some of the waterfalls listed are very remote with no cellular phone service and very little foot traffic. If you're injured, it could take a while to be found. With this in mind, it's always a good idea to let someone know your waterfall itinerary.

During the spring season or after heavy rainfall, the rivers are usually flowing very high and fast moving. Do not attempt to cross rivers and stay away from the river's edge. The water, even when shallow, can be incredibly powerful and can knock you off your feet. If you decide to creek walk or cross a stream or a river, use good judgment, and when in doubt, simply turn around.

What to Bring

Drinking water and snacks. There are no vending machines in the wilderness.

GPS and backup compass. A few waterfalls listed here are very hard to find without GPS. It's also useful to track your travel path. (Don't forget spare batteries.)

First-aid kit. You never know when accidents will happen. Be prepared.

Detailed area maps or an Upper Michigan atlas. Having a map is always handy for visualizing driving directions. With limited cellular service, using your phone for navigation isn't always reliable. Also, some mapping apps provide incorrect directions or road names.

Rubber boots or hip waders. These are helpful to get different views of the waterfalls. Also, a few of the waterfalls listed do require river/stream crossings.

Bug repellent/head net. There's nothing worse than forgetting the bug spray while out viewing the waterfalls. The typical culprits will be mosquitoes, black flies, stable flies and wood ticks.

Flashlight. Sometimes trips can take longer than expected. You don't want to be in the dark.

Survival pack. For the longer treks or more remote locations, it's always good to pack additional items if your trip turns for the worse. Items like waterproof matches, extra clothing, a knife or multi-tool and rope are always good to carry.

Cell phone and a backup battery charger. As mentioned, cellular phone coverage is limited around the Upper Peninsula. But, if you're fortunate to be in an area with coverage and you find yourself in trouble, being able to call 911 for help is always good.

Photographing Waterfalls

Here are some general principles and a few tips to photographing waterfalls that I typically follow. These can be applied to all levels of photographing ability and camera types.

Lighting. Because you're dealing with water, a bright sunny day can make for a bad day of photographing waterfalls. A bright, overhead sun can create stark contrasts and extreme highlights. A few times when out photographing, I have waited for a lone cloud to pass by, or I plan my trips by going in the early morning or late afternoon when the lighting is less harsh. So don't rule out a cloudy day or a rainy one. With the right protective gear, you can get some great shots with a wet landscape surrounding the waterfall.

Shutter Speed. More often than not, I prefer to showcase the water flowing smoothly (or a blurred motion effect) in photographs of waterfalls. To do this, I adjust my camera settings so the shutter speed is slower than say 1/2 of a second but I typically try for 1 second (or longer depending on how bright the light is). If you want to capture the water in detail as it's flowing over the drop, then shooting a fast shutter speed like 1/250th will get those results. (Note: With either of these types of shutter speed, you're also going to be adjusting your aperture and ISO speed.)

Tripod. If you're going after the blurred motion effect (as mentioned above), then you're also going to need a sturdy tripod. It is crucial that the camera does not move when the shutter is open. Tripods come in also sorts of sizes and budgets, so do a little research before purchasing. To go along with this, you may want to get a cable release or use the self-timer on your camera to release the shutter and capture the image. You would be amazed how much the camera moves if you're trying to depress the button on the camera itself.

Perspective. When I'm out photographing waterfalls, I'm always looking at the waterfall from a variety of angles or perspectives. If the river conditions permit, I will wear hip waders along the edge of the river or wade to the center of the river and see how it looks from there. Sometimes just lowering your tripod a few feet can create a very visually appealing scene. Or do the opposite, and step back away from the falls. Some of my favorite photos I have created were taken with the waterfall from afar or slightly through the trees.

Have Fun & Enjoy. Don't forget to take in and enjoy the scene. As you'll find, Michigan has some incredible waterfalls in some incredible locations and surrounded by awesome nature. Relax, have fun, enjoy the sights and sounds . . . make memories.

How to Use This Book

This book covers the entire state of Michigan and is organized geographically. The state is divided into seven regions: Eastern U.P., Central U.P., the Huron Mountains, Southern U.P., Western U.P., the Keweenaw Peninsula, and the Black River Scenic Byway/The Porcupine Mountains. For an overview map with all of the falls, see page 14.

Within each region, the falls are ranked according to three general categories: Top 22, Must-See, and Other Falls. As you might expect, the Top 22 Falls are the best waterfalls the state has to offer, and these entries include four pages and a large photograph to show off these falls' beauty and power. The Must-See Falls are wonderful falls in their own right, as are the Other Falls, which only get shorter shrift to keep the book from expanding to five volumes. And if you just can't get enough, head to page 224 and you'll find a table with 21 More Waterfalls to Explore.

Of course, my rankings are subjective, and you may disagree with them. When it comes down to it, the state simply has too many wonderful waterfalls. That's a great problem to have.

In each section of the book, I include the following information for each waterfall:

Location: Where the waterfall is located; usually this is a park or other natural area. The approximate location is marked on the map to the left.

Address/GPS for the Falls: The street address of the falls, if possible. If that's not an option, the address for the park is listed. The GPS coordinates for the actual falls are also listed, though keep in mind that you can't drive right up to many falls. A short hike is often required, so don't plug this into the GPS of your car.

Directions: General driving directions to reach the falls.

Website: The website for the site if one exists.

Waterway: The river or stream that produces the falls; some falls are located along unnamed streams/rivers.

Nearest Town: The nearest town/city.

Height: The approximate height of the falls, though this can be difficult to measure for slowly sloping rapids.

Crest: The width of the falls; this can vary quite a bit depending on the season and rainfall patterns.

Hike Difficulty: How strenuous the hike is overall.

Trail Quality: How well marked and secure your footing is on the trail; often includes details about trail surface, obstacles and steps/stairs.

Round-trip Distance: The distance you'll need to hike from your car to the falls and back.

Admission: Some waterfalls are located in settings that charge admission. Fee information is listed here, as applicable.

A number of the falls in this book are in Michigan State Parks, so you'll need a Michigan Recreation Passport to enter. For residents, annual vehicle passes are $11 if you purchase one when renewing your license plate or $16 if you purchase one at the state park's office. For non-residents, an annual permit costs $32; daily passes are $9. For details, visit the Michigan Department of Natural Resources website: www.michigan.gov/dnr

Trip Report & Tips: A step-by-step account of my visit to the falls, including detailed directions to reach the falls and information about how to get a closer look, if you're feeling adventurous. Trip reports also include interesting sights and attractions to look out for on the way, possible hazards, recommendations, and the best times to visit the falls.

81, 87
85
84
86
78
77, 80, 83
42, 47
93
64, 68
88
44-46
96
69
90
37, 40
35
25, 32
91
94
56
89
76
33
6, 17
5
92
82
26, 34
61
79
52
55
36
21
8-9, 11
12
62
95
97
51
75
19
1
70
65
50
22-23
27
18
10
71
53
7
15
4
63
57
58
30
24, 31
13-14, 16
66, 72
39, 43
67
28-29
73-74
38, 49
59
2
41, 48
60
3
54
20

Map of Michigan's Waterfalls

● Top 22 ● Must-See ● Other

Chapel Falls

Pictured Rocks National Lakeshore was established in 1966—the United States' first National Lakeshore.

View from platform past small bridge

Chapel Falls

I highly recommend continuing the hike to Chapel Beach to see the unique Chapel Rock along the Lake Superior shoreline.

LOCATION: Pictured Rocks National Lakeshore

ADDRESS/GPS FOR THE FALLS: 46° 31.718′ N, 86° 26.633′ W

DIRECTIONS: Take H-58 east from Munising for 14 miles. Turn left onto Chapel Dr., and drive 5 miles to the parking area at the end of the road.

WEBSITE: www.nps.gov/piro

WATERWAY: Section Thirtyfour Creek

HEIGHT: 65 feet **CREST:** 10–25 feet

NEAREST TOWN: Melstrand

HIKE DIFFICULTY: Fairly flat with some small hills

TRAIL QUALITY: Good; flat, even trail

ROUND-TRIP DISTANCE: 2.6 miles

ADMISSION: No fee

TRIP REPORT & TIPS:

Centrally located in the Pictured Rocks National Lakeshore, this parking area is the perfect jumping-off point when visiting the lakeshore. Besides visiting Chapel Falls, you can continue hiking to Lake Superior and Chapel Rock, or take the Chapel Loop, a great, long hike to see the towering sandstone cliffs. And finally, the hike to Mosquito Falls (page 46) is to the west.

As for the Chapel Falls hike, it is a pleasant walk on a nice path through towering hardwoods. Along the way, there is a spot to see nearby Chapel Lake. Once you arrive at the falls, you're standing at the crest, and a nearby platform gives a nice perspective from the side. Follow the creek upstream to see a picturesque, small upper falls with a footbridge. There, you can cross to see the other side of the falls and a nice view of the gorge that Chapel Falls flows into before it disappears into the wilderness. If you stay on the trail a bit farther, there is another platform view of the falls, looking back toward the south. This view gives a nice, straight-on perspective. At this point, you can either continue on the trail to Lake Superior and the Pictured Rocks shoreline or head back to the parking area.

Note: The parking area has nice pit toilets but no running water.

A beautiful upper falls just upstream

Lower Tahquamenon Falls

Lower Tahquamenon Falls is made up of five waterfalls. A small island divides the river and helps create these unique falls.

Lower Tahquamenon Falls 1

Lower Tahquamenon Falls 2, view from island

Lower Tahquamenon Falls

There is so much to do at the Lower Falls State Park including camping, fishing, canoeing, hiking and wading in the falls.

LOCATION: Tahquamenon Falls State Park

ADDRESS/GPS FOR THE FALLS: 41382 W. M-123, Paradise / 1: 46° 36.157' N, 85° 12.345' W; 2: 46° 36.246' N, 85° 12.385' W; 3: 46° 36.265' N, 85° 12.412' W; 4: 46° 36.225' N, 85° 12.432' W; 5: 46° 36.138' N, 85° 12.435' W

DIRECTIONS: From Newberry, drive north and then east on M-123 for 27 miles. Turn right at the entrance for the lower falls and campground.

WEBSITE: www.michigandnr.com/parksandtrails/Details.aspx?type=SPRK&id=428

WATERWAY: Tahquamenon River

HEIGHT: 1: 20 feet; 2: 9 feet; 3: 8 feet; 4: 5 feet; 5: 3 feet

CREST: 1: 130 feet; 2: 30 feet; 3: 88 feet; 4: 128 feet; 5: 210 feet

NEAREST TOWN: Paradise

HIKE DIFFICULTY: Easy, some stairs on the island

TRAIL QUALITY: Good

ROUND-TRIP DISTANCE: 1 mile; island and riverside observation decks

ADMISSION: Michigan Recreation Passport required (see page 12); rowboat rental

TRIP REPORT & TIPS:

I have to be honest, I don't know why I didn't visit Lower Tahquamenon Falls sooner! To me, the Lower Falls is truly a fun adventure for the entire family. During my visit, I brought along our 5-year-old daughter and she had a great time despite the rain. Our favorite part was renting a rowboat (for a small amount) and rowing the 150 yards to the nearby island in the middle of the river. Once you reach there and dock, a 0.5-mile trail follows the perimeter of the island, giving you close-up views of the cascading waterfalls that make up the Lower Falls. The river was running high during our visit, but during the midsummer, the falls are a popular place to wade and play in the water.

On our return to the mainland, we rowed around a bit, took in the views, and saw people trying their luck with fishing. Back on the riverbank, we followed the boardwalk trail along the north channel to see what the falls looked like from the two different observation decks. They were enjoyable but definitely not as fun as rowing to the island and seeing them from there!

Here's a breakdown of the falls as noted on one of the park's maps. To help you figure out which is which, I've made Falls 1 the first falls you see after walking from the parking lot. Then they're counter-clockwise from there.

Lower Tahquamenon Falls 1: This is the main double-drop cascading falls you see from a distance when walking from the parking lot. On the island, a large observation deck gives you a nice close-up view.

Lower Tahquamenon Falls 3

Lower Tahquamenon Falls 4, view from island

Lower Tahquamenon Falls 5, view from island

TRIP REPORT (CONTINUED): **Lower Tahquamenon Falls 2:** Located in the north channel, this narrow multi-level cascade is best viewed from the island, as it's closer to that side of the river. The layers of sandstone make for easy access to play in the water.

Lower Tahquamenon Falls 3: A small island splits this falls from falls 2, with this cascade being closer to the riverbank side. A large observation deck on the riverbank provides a great straight-on view of the falls. During the warm months, the base of the falls is a hotspot for those looking to cool off and play in the river. The observation deck is about 0.4 mile from the concessions building.

Lower Tahquamenon Falls 4: Located in the north channel, this smaller drop is upstream from falls 2 and 3. From the island, it's visible through the trees, and on the riverbank there's a small observation deck next to it. I enjoyed taking photos from the riverbank side, because the jaggedness of the drop seemed to be more visible from that side. It is about 80 yards between the two observation decks.

Lower Tahquamenon Falls 5: This is a small drop that is upstream from the island and before the river divides into channels. It is only really visible from the island and not that impressive.

I highly recommend renting a rowboat and navigating to the island

Upper Tahquamenon Falls

Upper Tahquamenon Falls is Michigan's most visited waterfall and one of the largest east of the Mississippi River. No matter the season, it's worth a visit.

An impressive view through the trees from the paved path

Upper Tahquamenon Falls

The visible brown streaks of water naturally occur from tannin which flows from upstream cedar swamps.

LOCATION: Tahquamenon Falls State Park

ADDRESS/GPS FOR THE FALLS: 41382 W. M-123, Paradise / 46° 34.509′ N, 85° 15.384′ W

DIRECTIONS: From Newberry, drive north on M-123 for 23 miles. The state park entrance will be on the right.

WEBSITE: www.michigandnr.com/parksandtrails/Details.aspx?type=SPRK&id=428

WATERWAY: Tahquamenon River

HEIGHT: 42 feet **CREST:** 202 feet

NEAREST TOWN: Paradise

HIKE DIFFICULTY: Easy

TRAIL QUALITY: Paved path and handicapped accessible; some viewing areas have stairs

ROUND-TRIP DISTANCE: 1 mile (from the parking lot to the observation deck and back)

ADMISSION: Michigan Recreation Passport required (see page 12)

TRIP REPORT & TIPS:

Upper Tahquamenon Falls is Michigan's most popular and well-known water-fall. After visiting here, you will understand why! It may not be the tallest, but it's a pretty grand display throughout the seasons. I highly recommend making a visit during the winter months, too. The parking area is plowed, and area snowmobile trails also pass through the area.

After parking, just follow the wide paved path into the woods. Along the way, you'll come to a split. I like to head to the right first. The thundering sound of Tahquamenon Falls will soon come into play before you see the falls. There are two great lookout points to check out. They provide the first glimpses of this beautiful falls. These are some of my favorite spots to photograph. Continuing on will take you to the top of a large staircase. This leads down to a large observation deck, right at the waterfall's crest. It is truly magnificent to get so close!

If you follow the paved trail back and continue along the top of the gorge, you'll get some nice glimpses of the falls straight on. Another large staircase takes you to the river's edge downstream of the falls. A boardwalk then leads to a viewing area that gives you a good perspective of how big a waterfall this is.

After your visit to the falls, the concessions area is also worth checking out. It has a restaurant with its own brewery, a gift shop, and a deck area with an outdoor fireplace.

Don't miss a visit during the winter

Miners Falls

A trip to Munising isn't complete without a visit to the iconic Miners Castle, a unique rock formation just a short drive from Miners Falls.

The treacherous climb to the base gets you this view

Miners Falls

The walk to Miners Falls is especially beautiful in the spring with an abundance of wildflowers lining the trail. The main road in is also a great spot to find wild trilliums.

LOCATION: Pictured Rocks National Lakeshore

ADDRESS/GPS FOR THE FALLS: 46° 28.493′ N, 86° 31.908′ W

DIRECTIONS: Take H-58 east out of Munising for 5 miles. Turn left onto Miners Castle Rd., and drive 3.7 miles and turn right onto the dirt road marked with a sign for the falls. Drive 0.5 mile to the parking area.

WEBSITE: www.nps.gov/piro

WATERWAY: Miners River

HEIGHT: 39 feet **CREST:** 15 feet

NEAREST TOWN: Munising

HIKE DIFFICULTY: Easy

TRAIL QUALITY: Maintained gravel trail with stairs at the end

ROUND-TRIP DISTANCE: 1.2 miles

ADMISSION: None

TRIP REPORT & TIPS:

Miners Falls is a very impressive waterfall and should be on your list to visit, especially since it's conveniently located near the iconic Miners Castle rock formation. The walk begins on a well-maintained path through the forest, surrounded by towering trees. During the spring season, a carpet of wildflowers fills the forest here, and they are especially beautiful. Near the end of the walk, you'll begin to hear the sound of the waterfall, and two viewing options are available. The first option is blocked by trees, so you're better off heading down the stairs. The sight and sound you're greeted with is pretty powerful. Depending on the water levels and wind, the spray coming off the falls can get you a bit wet here, but it's worth it!

There is no footpath to the bottom of the waterfall (and the park doesn't recommend it), and the trip down can be very slippery and muddy. Please use extra caution if you decide to venture down.

At the parking area, there is RV/camper parking and pit toilets. Along the trail, there are benches if you need a rest. No pets are allowed on the trail.

Snowmobile, ski or snowshoe for a winter visit

Spray Falls

Spray Falls might be one of the most picturesque waterfalls on Lake Superior. The towering sandstone cliffs of Pictured Rocks help create this wonderful scene.

The impressive view from the Lakeshore Trail

Spray Falls

During the winter months, the sandstone cliffs of Pictured Rocks become a playground for ice climbers. Water leeching through the rock freezes and creates giant curtains of ice.

LOCATION: Pictured Rocks National Lakeshore

ADDRESS/GPS FOR THE FALLS: 46° 33.477′N, 86° 24.634′W

DIRECTIONS: The falls are viewable from Lake Superior by boat or via hiking. If you're hiking, from Munising, drive east on H-58 for 19 miles. Turn left on Little Beaver Lake Rd., and drive 2.7 miles to the parking area.

WEBSITE: www.nps.gov/piro

WATERWAY: Spray Creek

HEIGHT: 76 feet **CREST:** 25 feet

NEAREST TOWN: Grand Marais

HIKE DIFFICULTY: Moderate

TRAIL QUALITY: Good, but some hills and tree roots

ROUND-TRIP DISTANCE: 7.4 miles

ADMISSION: No fee

TRIP REPORT & TIPS:

Spray Falls might be one of the most dramatic waterfalls that flows into Lake Superior. Situated along Lake Superior and the towering sandstone cliffs of Pictured Rocks, this falls is a sheer drop into the big lake and a very impressive sight!

Spray Falls is unique in that you can enjoy it from land or on the water. The fastest and easiest way to see the falls is from the water, taking the Pictured Rocks Cruise. They offer a special Spray Falls cruise that goes farther up the shoreline to see this falls. You also have the option to rent a pontoon boat from local outfitters and navigate the lake yourself to see the falls.

Viewing it by land requires a lengthy hike, but it's well worth the effort. Along the hike to the falls, you'll pass some great scenery, including views of the Lake Superior shoreline, with its unique sandstone rock formations. After parking near Little Beaver Lake Campground, you'll first have to hike to the shoreline for 1.4 miles. Parts of this section can be muddy, and there are some small hills. Once you reach the shoreline, head west on the Lakeshore Trail, which is also part of the North Country Trail. The terrain starts off relatively flat but then becomes more hilly as the cliffs rise above Lake Superior. After 2.3 miles, you'll see a small sign noting Spray Falls and a trail leading to the right. This short side trail leads you to an amazing clearing along Pictured Rocks that is also high above the water. From here you can see Spray Falls (about 300+ yards away) and the rest of the impressive shoreline.

Note: There are no barriers or fences along the trails, so make sure to watch your footing as well as keep small children away from the edge.

A stunning sight

Best viewing in the spring and early summer

Bridalveil Falls

LOCATION: Pictured Rocks National Lakeshore

ADDRESS/GPS FOR THE FALLS: 46° 30.521' N, 86° 31.393' W

DIRECTIONS: 0.5 mile east of Miners Beach, along the Pictured Rocks cliffs and best viewed from the lake.

WEBSITE: www.nps.gov/piro

WATERWAY: Unnamed creek

HEIGHT: 157 feet **CREST:** 4–7 feet

NEAREST TOWN: Munising

HIKE DIFFICULTY: Best viewed from Lake Superior

TRAIL QUALITY: N/A

ROUND-TRIP DISTANCE: N/A

ADMISSION: You'll need to charter a boat or bring a sea kayak.

TRIP REPORT & TIPS:

At 157 feet, Bridalveil Falls is Michigan's tallest waterfall. This unique waterfall flows down the face of the Pictured Rocks cliffs and into Lake Superior, making it a unique sight. As you might guess, it is best viewed from the water, by boat or kayak. Luckily, there are a few options available in Munising. The quickest and easiest is taking the Pictured Rocks Cruises boat tour, which travels along the shoreline and features a narrated tour of the towering cliffs, as well as this waterfall. If you're feeling more adventurous or have more time, you can rent a pontoon boat and navigate there yourself along the shoreline, or take a guided sea kayak trip. There are several outfitters in the area offering these water treks.

Bridalveil Falls can also be a seasonal waterfall and slow down to a trickle during the hot, dry summer months. During my visit in October, the flow was minimal, as seen in the photo.

Laughing Whitefish Falls

LOCATION: Laughing Whitefish Falls Scenic Site

ADDRESS/GPS FOR THE FALLS: 46° 23.018′ N, 87° 04.144′ W

DIRECTIONS: From Chatham, drive west on M-94 for 7.7 miles to Sundell Rd. Take a right (north) onto N. Sundell Rd., and drive 2 miles. The road will turn to the right, but continue straight onto the dirt road. Continue on the dirt road for 0.3 mile, and turn right at the marked DNR sign. Keep following the road 0.4 mile to the parking area.

WEBSITE: www.michigan.gov/dnr/0,4570,7-153-31154_31260-54016--,00.html

WATERWAY: Laughing Whitefish River

HEIGHT: 95 feet, initial 15-foot drop with fanning cascade **CREST:** 20 feet

NEAREST TOWN: Sundell

HIKE DIFFICULTY: Easy; small hills

TRAIL QUALITY: Good

ROUND-TRIP DISTANCE: 1 mile

ADMISSION: Michigan Recreation Passport required (see page 12)

TRIP REPORT & TIPS:

Laughing Whitefish Falls might not get a lot of attention, because of its secluded location, but it definitely packs a punch in terms of size and accessibility. This Michigan DNR Scenic Site is well maintained, with a crushed stone path, which makes it a fun family adventure. The path is fairly flat, with a slight descent and a few small hills through an open forest of maple, beech, and cedar trees. Along the way there are benches if you need to take a rest. When you reach the falls, you are at the top of the waterfall, and a large platform provides a great view of the falls and gorge. If you're up for stairs, a large staircase will first guide you to a viewing area, where you can see the initial 15-foot drop of the falls and hollowed caves in the limestone rock. From there, you can continue down more stairs to the bottom of the waterfall. The view at the bottom isn't the best, because of the trees, so many folks climb over the railing and down to the river to get head-on photos of the falls. In total, the staircases have 153 steps. If you plan to explore the river or walk up the cascade, the limestone can be slippery, so use caution.

At the parking area, there is a pit toilet, picnic table, barbeque grill, and a hand-pump well for water. No camping is allowed.

Memorial Falls

LOCATION: City of Munising

ADDRESS/GPS FOR THE FALLS: 46° 25.058′ N, 86° 37.648′ W

DIRECTIONS: Follow H-58 east out of Munising and turn right onto Nestor St., just a short distance past Washington St., which goes to Sand Point. Drive one block and turn left to park along Cleveland St.

WEBSITE: www.michigannature.org

WATERWAY: Memorial Creek

HEIGHT: 46 feet **CREST:** 4 feet

NEAREST TOWN: Munising

HIKE DIFFICULTY: Fair

TRAIL QUALITY: A narrow trail with roots and rocks

ROUND-TRIP DISTANCE: 0.2 mile; from Olson Falls: 0.6 mile

ADMISSION: No fee; no dogs allowed

TRIP REPORT & TIPS:

After parking, continue walking down Nestor St. to the trailhead on the right. Follow the trail into the woods, and you'll soon forget you're within the city limits of Munising. A fairly decent trail winds through the trees, and soon you'll cross a small footbridge over a stream, giving you your first sight of the falls. Here you are standing at the top of the falls. Continuing on the trail (look for the blue markers), head to the right where the trail backtracks and descends along a fenced ridge. The trail can be narrow at times in the beginning, but then it widens along the base of a sandstone cliff, which has some very interesting shapes. Arriving at the falls, a pretty thin stream of water flowing over the edge greets you as it splashes down into a very shallow pool.

This falls is also worth a visit during the winter months. You may need some snowshoes, but the sight of the frozen waterfall as a giant ice pillar is pretty cool (no pun intended).

Nearby Olson Falls (Tannery Falls) (page 44) is also worth the visit. It requires a little more effort and hiking distance but is very close by. The land for both of these falls is owned and maintained by the Michigan Nature Association.

Olson Falls *(Tannery Falls)*

LOCATION: City of Munising

ADDRESS/GPS FOR THE FALLS: 46° 24.951′ N, 86° 37.612′ W

DIRECTIONS: Follow H-58 east out of Munising and turn right on Nestor St., just a short distance past Washington St. which goes to Sand Point. Drive one block and turn left to park along Cleveland St.

WEBSITE: www.michigannature.org

WATERWAY: Tannery Creek

HEIGHT: 38 feet **CREST:** 8 feet

NEAREST TOWN: Munising

HIKE DIFFICULTY: Fair; some hills

TRAIL QUALITY: Good

ROUND-TRIP DISTANCE: From parking lot: 0.8 mile; from Memorial Falls: 0.6 mile

ADMISSION: No fee; no dogs allowed

TRIP REPORT & TIPS:

Formerly known as Tannery Falls, Olson Falls is part of the Twin Waterfalls Nature Sanctuary. Memorial Falls (page 42) is also part of the sanctuary. Because of its location and the effort it takes to get to the falls, Tannery is the less popular of the two. With that said, getting there is part of the fun. The narrow paths, a few hills, and bit more distance make it feel much wilder and challenging.

After visiting Memorial Falls, you're going to want to follow the alternate trail (marked with blue markers), which heads south and away from the trail heading back to the trailhead. This will take you down a large hill, and near the bottom (close to H-58) there will be a staircase to your left. Here, the trail markers will be green. Follow this and the trail will lead you up and along the ridge of a sandstone canyon. The trail will lead along a hillside, and Olson Falls will come into view. As you get closer to the falls, the trail will continue to the bottom, which is a fun experience! A convenient footbridge crosses the creek, and you can then explore and learn a bit about the history of the area from nearby signage. Continue on the trail, and it will lead you back to the base of the hill and near H-58, completing the loop.

Lower falls; the upper falls is just upstream.

Mosquito Falls

LOCATION: Pictured Rocks National Lakeshore

ADDRESS/GPS FOR THE FALLS: 46° 31.013′ N, 86° 28.704′ W'

DIRECTIONS: Drive H-58 east from Munising 14 miles. Turn left onto Chapel Rd., and drive 5 miles to the parking area at the end of the road.

WEBSITE: www.nps.gov/piro

WATERWAY: Mosquito River

HEIGHT: Upper and lower falls are each 8 feet **CREST:** 25 feet

NEAREST TOWN: Melstrand

HIKE DIFFICULTY: Moderate

TRAIL QUALITY: Roots, rocks, and steep grades

ROUND-TRIP DISTANCE: 2.4 miles

ADMISSION: No fee

TRIP REPORT & TIPS:

Compared to the nearby trek to Chapel Falls, Mosquito Falls has more of a wild feel to it, as it's less traveled and the terrain is a little more difficult. The reward of reaching the falls is very gratifying, though. The falls feature two nice drops, with a nice set of rapids and cascades in between. The lower falls are in a small gorge and are a straight drop. The upper falls have more level terrain around and feature a cascade over large, jagged rocks.

The hike begins by heading toward the northwest, with signs guiding you along the way. The beginning of the hike has more gentle slopes and then transitions into a few steeper hills, but nothing too crazy in my opinion. Once you're near the river, you follow a ridge to the lower falls. This puts you at the top of the falls. From there you can follow the river upstream for 150 yards to the upper falls.

As with Chapel Falls, you also have the option to continue on the trail past the falls to the Lake Superior shoreline and the cliffs of Pictured Rocks.

The view from the main platform

Munising Falls

LOCATION: Pictured Rocks National Lakeshore

ADDRESS/GPS FOR THE FALLS: 1505 Sand Point Rd., Munising / 46° 25.372' N, 86° 37.308' W

DIRECTIONS: From Munising, take H-58 east for 1.3 miles. Turn left onto Washington St. Continue for 0.6 mile, and there's a large parking lot on the right side with a small visitor's center building. Munising Memorial Hospital is across the street.

WEBSITE: www.nps.gov/piro

WATERWAY: Munising Falls Creek

HEIGHT: 50 feet **CREST:** 5 feet

NEAREST TOWN: Munising

HIKE DIFFICULTY: Easy

TRAIL QUALITY: Good; an ADA-accessible asphalt path

ROUND-TRIP DISTANCE: 0.4 mile

ADMISSION: No fee; pets are allowed on the trail

TRIP REPORT & TIPS:

Munising Falls is likely the most visited waterfall of Pictured Rocks National Lakeshore. The waterfall is close to town and has a paved path, making it easily accessible. The walk to the falls is pleasant as it follows Munising Falls Creek upstream and winds through the forest. When you reach the small bridge, the falls come into view, and the sound of the rushing water echoes off the sandstone canyon walls. At the end of the main path, there's a large viewing platform and a bench to help take in the scenery. There are also two other views of the falls; both require some stairs, but this main platform is the best of the three. If you're feeling adventurous, the set of stairs before the bridge is worth the climb. Along that route you'll also pass by some unique sandstone features in the cliffs.

During the winter months, the waterfall is also worth checking out. The parking lot is plowed, but the path leading to it is not maintained. The few times I've visited during the winter, there has been enough foot traffic to pack down a decent path. The waterfall freezes, leaving a giant ice pillar, but you can hear the sound of water flowing through the center of it—a pretty cool experience!

Sable Falls

LOCATION: Pictured Rocks National Lakeshore

ADDRESS/GPS FOR THE FALLS: 46° 40.116′ N, 86° 00.848′ W

DIRECTIONS: From Grand Marais, drive west on H-58 for 1.4 miles. The sign and driveway are on the right side.

WEBSITE: www.nps.gov/piro

WATERWAY: Sable Creek

HEIGHT: 52 feet **CREST:** 35 feet

NEAREST TOWN: Grand Marais

HIKE DIFFICULTY: Easy, but with stairs

TRAIL QUALITY: Maintained trail with stairs

ROUND-TRIP DISTANCE: 0.6 mile

ADMISSION: No fee; pets only allowed in parking lot/picnic area

TRIP REPORT & TIPS:

Sable Falls isn't your typical stop, because the area offers much more than a great waterfall. The nearby Grand Sable Dunes begin just to the west of the falls, and a nearby trail can take you to explore this unusual landscape. Also nearby is the picturesque Lake Superior shoreline, which you can see if you continue on the path after seeing Sable Falls.

From the large parking lot, head north on the paved trail toward the falls; you'll see the newly built restrooms on the right. The approach to the falls is from the top, so there is a very large wooden staircase (169 steps) to descend in order to see the waterfall. (There are benches along the way should you get tired.) The waterfall itself is impressive. The water flows over two consecutive drops and is sort of funneled by the carved rock, before it makes a few more cascades. As I mentioned earlier about Lake Superior, you'll want to continue on the path as it follows Sable Creek to the big lake. The trail becomes a dirt path with a few small stairs. At the beach, you'll get to see the steep, towering Grand Sable Dunes as they hug the shoreline to the west.

Photo taken along the river's edge

Wagner Falls

LOCATION: Munising

ADDRESS/GPS FOR THE FALLS: 46° 23.281′ N, 86° 38.839′ W

DIRECTIONS: From Munising, head east 1 mile on M-28. Turn right onto M-94. The falls parking area is just ahead, on the left after 0.3 mile.

WEBSITE: None

WATERWAY: Wagner Creek

HEIGHT: 28 feet **CREST:** 20 feet

NEAREST TOWN: Munising

HIKE DIFFICULTY: Easy

TRAIL QUALITY: Good; a groomed trail with a wooden boardwalk and steps to a viewing platform at the end

ROUND-TRIP DISTANCE: 0.2 mile

ADMISSION: Michigan Recreation Passport required (see page 12)

TRIP REPORT & TIPS:

Wagner Falls might be one of Munising's most popular waterfalls, and for good reason—it's a beautiful setting and close to town. The walk begins on a well-maintained path that then becomes a wooden boardwalk. Just before reaching the falls, a small brook on the right provides a picturesque scene as it flows out of the forest. Continue up the stairs, and you reach the viewing platform overlooking the multiple drops that make up Wagner Falls. During the early summer, marsh marigolds provide some nice color along the banks. Many folks will also visit during the winter months, as the area is very pretty after a snowfall. Your best bet for that is early winter, as it tends to freeze/ice over as the winter progresses.

There is also another waterfall a little farther upstream, Upper Wagner Falls. It is much smaller and less dramatic than the main one. There's also no trail and the hillsides are slippery/muddy, so unless you're a die-hard waterfall enthusiast, it isn't worth the effort. Instead, take a seat on the bench and enjoy the sights and sounds of Wagner Falls.

Alger Falls

LOCATION: Roadside east of Munising

ADDRESS/GPS FOR THE FALLS: Roadside on M-28 East / 46° 23.592′ N, 86° 38.891′ W

DIRECTIONS: From downtown Munising, head east out of town on M-28 for 4 miles. The waterfall is located along the highway and across from the M-94 intersection.

WEBSITE: None

WATERWAY: Alger Creek

HEIGHT: 21 feet **CREST:** 8–10 feet

NEAREST TOWN: Munising

HIKE DIFFICULTY: N/A

TRAIL QUALITY: N/A

ROUND-TRIP DISTANCE: N/A

ADMISSION: No fee

TRIP REPORT & TIPS:

It can be easy to miss this roadside waterfall, as it's a little tucked into the woods, if you're driving west toward Munising. But it's worth the stop, as it's easy to view and a wide shoulder provides enough parking along the busy highway. If you're looking to get out and explore a little, expect some muddy footpaths created by previous visitors. The area leading to the base of the falls is usually very marshy throughout the year. If it's a bright, sunny day, I recommend photographing these falls in the late afternoon or evening, as the waterfall faces west.

Lower Au Train Falls

LOCATION: Au Train

ADDRESS/GPS FOR THE FALLS: N5030 Power Dam Rd., Au Train / 46° 20.337′ N, 86° 51.114′ W

DIRECTIONS: From Munising, take M-94 west for 12 miles. Turn right onto Au Train Rd. After 0.1 mile, take a right on unpaved Power Dam Rd. Follow that for 0.4 mile to the parking lot at the gate for the Lower Falls. The Upper Falls parking area is 0.2 mile from the paved road. The area is marked with a sign detailing the layout of the hydroelectric dam.

WEBSITE: None

WATERWAY: Au Train River

HEIGHT: 15 feet **CREST:** 45 feet

NEAREST TOWN: Au Train

HIKE DIFFICULTY: Moderate

TRAIL QUALITY: A dirt road with a hill

ROUND-TRIP DISTANCE: 0.2 mile

ADMISSION: No fee

TRIP REPORT & TIPS:

From the parking area, walk past the gate and down the dirt road heading to the lower falls. You'll reach a large wooden bridge, which gives you a great view of the falls and the many layers of rock underlying them. Typically, the river levels are low enough that you can walk around in the water and play in the river. The green moss, though, can be slippery, so just watch your step. In recent years, they've also added a picnic area near the lower falls. I found this to be great place for a lunch break before heading to see other falls.

Horseshoe Falls

LOCATION: Munising

ADDRESS/GPS FOR THE FALLS:
602 Bell Ave., Munising, MI 49864 / 46° 24.176' N, 86° 38.569' W

DIRECTIONS: Drive east on M-28 out of Munising, and turn left onto Prospect St. Drive 2 blocks and follow the road to the left, where it becomes Bell Ave. The parking lot is at the end of the street.

WEBSITE: www.uppermichiganwaterfalls.com

WATERWAY: Unnamed creek

HEIGHT: 35 feet **CREST:** 4–12 feet

NEAREST TOWN: Munising

HIKE DIFFICULTY: Easy, slight hill to falls

TRAIL QUALITY: Good, groomed path

ROUND-TRIP DISTANCE: 0.2 mile

ADMISSION: $6/person; ages 4–12 $3/person

TRIP REPORT & TIPS:

Horseshoe Falls is a privately owned waterfall located within the city of Munising. Thankfully, the owners have turned it into a neat little attraction geared toward families. When I visited with my kids, they loved the place! Besides the waterfall, there is a fun gnome scavenger hunt, a large pond with rainbow trout you can feed, walking trails lined with unique items, and a nice gift shop.

As for the waterfall itself, it's similar to some of the others in the area but unique in its own way. Spring fed, it has a pretty consistent flow throughout the year. The walk to the falls is slightly uphill, so you get a nice view of the falls as the water flows over the horseshoe-shaped gorge and then makes its way down the hillside.

Elliot Falls *(Miners Beach Falls)*

LOCATION: Pictured Rocks National Lakeshore

ADDRESS/GPS FOR THE FALLS: East end of Miners Beach / 46° 29.988' N, 86° 31.900' W

DIRECTIONS: Take H-58 east out of Munising for 5 miles. Turn left onto Miners Castle Rd., and drive 5 miles to the "Y" and take a right. Go 1 mile to the stop sign. Turn right and continue to the parking area.

WEBSITE: www.nps.gov/piro

WATERWAY: Unnamed

HEIGHT: 4 feet **CREST:** 3 feet

NEAREST TOWN: Munising

HIKE DIFFICULTY: Easy

TRAIL QUALITY: Sandy

ROUND-TRIP DISTANCE: 0.4 mile

ADMISSION: No fee

TRIP REPORT & TIPS:

This waterfall may lack the height of others falls, but the setting is probably one of the most scenic in Michigan. From the parking area, head north toward Lake Superior on the sandy trail and continue the short distance until you reach Miners Beach. Once you reach the shoreline, look toward the right for a short overhanging rock shelf with a small stream flowing from the woods. The stream flows over the short rock shelf, lands on layers of sandstone rock, and finally heads into Lake Superior. The stretch of beach here is also one of my favorites, as the towering cliffs of Pictured Rocks National Lakeshore surround you. It's also a great place to take in a summer sunset.

Rock River Falls

LOCATION: Rock River Canyon Wilderness, Hiawatha National Forest

ADDRESS/GPS FOR THE FALLS: 46° 24.669′ N, 86° 58.560′ W

DIRECTIONS: From Chatham, drive north on Rock River Rd. for 3.3 miles to Sandstrom Rd. (Forest Rd. 2276). Turn left and follow the two-track road for 3.7 miles. Turn left onto Forest Road 2293, and continue 0.7 mile to the small parking area on left side of the road.

WEBSITE: None

WATERWAY: Rock River

HEIGHT: 19 feet **CREST:** 20 feet

NEAREST TOWN: Chatham

HIKE DIFFICULTY: Easy to moderate

TRAIL QUALITY: Smooth two-track at first, then narrow and can be muddy, with roots and rocks

ROUND-TRIP DISTANCE: 2 miles

ADMISSION: No fee

TRIP REPORT & TIPS:

Because of its remoteness, Rock River Falls doesn't get a lot of foot traffic. The trail begins as a wide two-track trail with a slight downhill grade. At about the halfway point, the trail becomes much narrower, and the forest becomes denser. In a few spots, there are wooden planks to help you cross wet areas, but the trail can still be muddy.

When you finally near the falls, they're hidden from view and the sound is muted by surrounding rocks. When it comes into view, it's very enchanting, as the natural light seems to shine down on it from the small opening in the trees above.

Scott Falls

LOCATION: Au Train

ADDRESS/GPS FOR THE FALLS: 46° 26.218′ N, 86° 48.878′ W

DIRECTIONS: From Munising, drive west 10.2 miles on M-28. The waterfall is on the left side of the road, hidden from view. Many park on the side of the road, where the shoulder is a bit wider. Across the road is a nice roadside park with access to Lake Superior.

WEBSITE: None

WATERWAY: Unnamed

HEIGHT: 11 feet **CREST:** 2 feet

NEAREST TOWN: Au Train

HIKE DIFFICULTY: Roadside

TRAIL QUALITY: Viewable from road, but a short wet trail leads to base of falls

ROUND-TRIP DISTANCE: Viewable from highway

ADMISSION: No fee

TRIP REPORT & TIPS:

No matter the season, this is a great waterfall to visit, as it's conveniently located next to the highway. This makes it highly accessible and viewable to all. During the winter months, the water will freeze into a nice, round ice column, but you'll still be able to hear the eerie but awesome sound of water flowing in the center. If you want to get a little closer, the trail to the base can be tricky (and wet), but it's definitely worth it. There is a small cavern behind the falls, which is also super fun to explore. Not bad for a roadside waterfall!

Ocqueoc Falls

LOCATION: Lower Peninsula, Ocqueoc Falls State Forest Campground

ADDRESS/GPS FOR THE FALLS: 45° 23.790′ N, 84° 03.472′ W

DIRECTIONS: Starting in Indian River, take M-68 east for 26.5 miles, passing through Onaway along the route. Turn left on S. Ocqueoc Rd., and drive north for 2.7 miles. Then turn right on Ocqueoc Falls Highway. Drive for 1.7 miles, and turn left into parking area for the falls, which is noted with a sign.

WEBSITE: www.michigandnr.com/ parksandtrails/details.aspx?id=627&type=SFCG

WATERWAY: Ocqueoc River

HEIGHT: 5 feet **CREST:** 42 feet

NEAREST TOWN: Millersburg

HIKE DIFFICULTY: Easy

TRAIL QUALITY: Paved

ROUND-TRIP DISTANCE: 0.2 mile

ADMISSION: Michigan Recreation Passport required (see page 12)

TRIP REPORT & TIPS:

Ocqueoc Falls is only waterfall located in the Lower Peninsula, and it is also the only universally accessible waterfall in the United States! On hot summer days you'll find visitors wading and swimming in the falls, which is encouraged. The falls is the highlight of the park, but there are also hiking paths, a great picnic area and campground.

After parking, just follow the concrete path which leads to the falls. Once at the river, there are a few different routes so everyone is able to enjoy this natural wonder.

Dead River Falls

Dead River Falls is a popular destination for local college students and thrill-seekers who cliff jump into the river.

Dead River Falls 1

Dead River Falls 2

Dead River Falls

At Dead River Falls, you'll instantly forget you're only a few minutes from town with its rugged and wild feel.

LOCATION: Marquette

ADDRESS/GPS FOR THE FALLS: 1: 46° 34.175′N, 87° 28.741′W; 2: 46° 34.155′N, 87° 28.732′W; 3: 46° 34.100′N, 87° 28.712′W; 4: 46° 34.090′N, 87° 28.737′W; 5: 46° 34.041′N, 87° 28.722′W; 6: 46° 33.995′N, 87° 28.827′W; 7: 46° 33.853′N, 87° 28.923′W

DIRECTIONS: From Marquette, travel west on US-41/M-28 to the stoplight where Target and Walmart are located. Turn right (north) onto Co. Rd. HQ, and drive for 0.7 mile to Forestville Rd. Turn left and follow Forestville Rd. for 2.2 miles to the end, where the road will make a loop. You will see a small parking area, an outhouse, and an old powerhouse building.

WEBSITE: None

WATERWAY: Dead River

HEIGHT: 1: 4 feet; 2: 14 feet; 3: 18 feet; 4: 17 feet; 5: 8.5 feet; 6: 24 feet 7: 16 feet

CREST: Varies

NEAREST TOWN: Marquette

HIKE DIFFICULTY: Difficult; steep hills, roots, rocks, narrow trails

TRAIL QUALITY: Rough, narrow, worn trails on steep grades

ROUND-TRIP DISTANCE: 1.8 miles to see all the falls

ADMISSION: No fee

TRIP REPORT & TIPS:

Locally, the Dead River Falls are well known, but they aren't as well known state-wide, and I'm not sure why. If you're looking for adventure and some amazing terrain close to town, this place is for you. The Dead River Falls are actually made up of several waterfalls. (I chose to highlight 7 waterfalls here, but you could actually count several more.) For a half mile, the river flows through a gorge of steep, rocky terrain and drops in elevation nearly 100 feet. Between the first waterfall and the last, you will discover some incredible spots to view the river—whether from a bluff or up close on jagged volcanic rock. Along the way, the river twists and turns through a forest of giant hemlocks, cedars, and pines.

What makes this trek adventurous and different from the other waterfalls is the hiking. It can be difficult at times, and extra caution is needed. The trails can be steep, narrow, precarious, and strenuous. I would say most can take on the conditions, but be advised just what you'll be taking on.

Dead River Falls 3

Dead River Falls 4

Dead River Falls 5

Dead River Falls 6

TRIP REPORT (CONTINUED): To get to the falls, you'll want to first hike up the steep gravel road beyond the gate. Once on top, follow the trail for a short distance, and then look for the staircase on the left leading into the woods. There are also a couple carved wooden signs to point you in the right direction. Follow the well-worn trail to the river, and the adventure begins. From the first small cascading falls, the trail follows the river upstream, and you'll encounter more falls along the way. After a half mile, you will reach a large plunging falls with the river widening and flattening above it. Continue on the trail a bit farther, and you will come to the last big waterfall, which has carved out the hillside.

Dead River Falls 7

West Branch Yellow Dog Falls

West Branch Yellow Dog Falls is the first waterfall you'll encounter on the Yellow Dog Falls hike in the northeast corner of the McCormick Wilderness.

There are also some nice some cascades just upstream from the main falls which are worth seeing

West Branch Yellow Dog Falls

Although there is a worn path from other visitors, there are no marked trails in the McCormick Wilderness. I highly recommend using a GPS for navigation and having a compass for backup.

LOCATION: McCormick Wilderness, Ottawa National Forest

ADDRESS/GPS FOR THE FALLS: 46° 43.351′ N, 87° 57.753′ W

DIRECTIONS: From Big Bay, drive south on Co. Rd. 550 (Big Bay Rd.) for 2 miles, then turn right onto Co. Rd. 510 for another 2.6 miles, where you will stay straight to follow the newly paved AAA Rd. Continue for another 7.9 miles, where the asphalt ends and the road switches to dirt. (The fenced mining property is to the right.) From here, keep heading west. At 4.9 miles, you will pass by Ford Rd. (unmarked) on the right, and then the AAA Rd. will veer sharply to the left shortly after that. From here, you are now on AAA Rd./Ford Rd. After 0.5 mile, AAA Rd. will turn right, but you'll want to continue straight (south) on Ford Rd. Stay on this main dirt road for another 1.5 miles. There will be a wide two-track road on the left, just after the "Trails End" hunting camp. Follow this for a couple hundred yards to the end, where signs note the McCormick Wilderness area.

WEBSITE: www.fs.usda.gov/recarea/ottawa/recarea/?recid=12361

WATERWAY: West Branch Yellow Dog River

HEIGHT: 35 feet **CREST:** 1–12 feet

NEAREST TOWN: Big Bay

HIKE DIFFICULTY: Moderate

TRAIL QUALITY: Fair, with some wet areas; trail

ROUND-TRIP DISTANCE: 2.2 miles

ADMISSION: None

TRIP REPORT & TIPS:

Located on the western edge of Marquette County, this waterfall is located within the McCormick Wilderness. This federally designated wilderness area has no marked trails or roads and is close to 17,000 acres. Because of the remoteness, the Forest Service asks that you self-register prior to your trip. Because the trails aren't marked and you're relying on prior foot traffic, I highly recommend having a fully charged GPS to navigate.

After you self-register, continue past the display board, and head down the narrow trail that's straight ahead; it's known as Yellow Dog Falls Trail. The trail makes its way through the forest and is fairly easy to follow. Along the way, I only found a couple spots where the trail seemed to disappear, but that was mostly near some wet areas. When the trail comes to the river, you should be able to hear the West Branch Yellow Dog Falls, as they are just a short distance upstream. A side trail follows the river upstream.

Here the landscape becomes very rugged and rocky. At the start of the falls, the river flows over a very nice, wide drop, and then the slanted bedrock pushes the water into a narrow, long slide, before it enters the waiting pool. After viewing this falls, make sure to continue upstream a short ways to see the upper portion. Here, the river cascades in an "S" shape down the hillside and along the edge of a very blocky, rugged riverbank on the opposite side.

After you make your way back to the "main" trail (where you first arrived at the river), you have the option to head back to your vehicle or wade the river to another series of waterfalls, the Yellow Dog Falls (Bulldog Falls) (page 72).

Yellow Dog Falls
(Bulldog Falls)

Located near the headwaters, this stretch of the river was designated as a "National Wild and Scenic River" by Congress in 1992.

The first and largest waterfall you'll encounter. The noted GPS coordinates are for this particular falls.

Yellow Dog Falls *(Bulldog Falls)*

The McCormick Wilderness features 16,925 acres of protected forest and was once a vacation getaway for the famous McCormick family—inventors of the reaping machine.

LOCATION: McCormick Wilderness, Ottawa National Forest

ADDRESS/GPS FOR THE FALLS: 46° 42.892′ N, 87° 57.114′ W

DIRECTIONS: From Big Bay, drive south on Co. Rd. 550 (Big Bay Rd.) for 2 miles, then turn right onto Co. Rd. 510 for another 2.6 miles, where you will stay straight to follow the newly paved AAA Rd. Continue for another 7.9 miles, where the asphalt ends and the road switches to dirt. (The fenced mining property is to the right.) From here, keep heading west. At 4.9 miles, you will pass by Ford Rd. (unmarked) on the right, and then the AAA Rd. will veer sharply to the left shortly after that. From here, you are now on AAA Rd./Ford Rd. After 0.5 mile, AAA Rd. will turn right, but you'll want to continue straight (south) on Ford Rd. Stay on this main dirt road for another 1.5 miles. There will be a wide two-track road on the left, just after the "Trails End" hunting camp. Follow this for a couple hundred yards to the end, where signs note the McCormick Wilderness area.

WEBSITE: www.fs.usda.gov/recarea/ottawa/recarea/?recid=12361

WATERWAY: Yellow Dog River

HEIGHT: 23 feet **CREST:** 15 feet

NEAREST TOWN: Big Bay

HIKE DIFFICULTY: Difficult, hilly terrain, with little to no trail

TRAIL QUALITY: Poor to none

ROUND-TRIP DISTANCE: 6.2 miles (from trailhead to final waterfall in series)

ADMISSION: None

TRIP REPORT & TIPS:

Yellow Dog Falls (also referred to as Bulldog Falls) is located in the rugged and wildly remote McCormick Wilderness. This federally designated wilderness area has no marked trails or roads and is close to 17,000 acres. Because of the remoteness, the Forest Service asks that you self-register prior to your trip. Because the trails aren't marked and you're relying on prior foot traffic, I highly recommend having a fully charged GPS to navigate.

From the trailhead, you're going to take the same trail as described for the West Branch falls. After a mile, you will come to the narrow West Branch River (about 10 feet wide, 12–18 inches deep), which you'll need to wade across to continue on to Yellow Dog Falls. Travel for 0.7 mile, and you will come to the main branch of the Yellow Dog River. From here, follow the river upstream for about 0.4 mile, where you will see an island within the river. (Look for ancient cedar footbridges to help you get to the island and then to the opposite side.)

At this point, the terrain becomes very rocky and more difficult to navigate. Follow the river upstream (on the east bank) from here, to see roughly 7–8 waterfalls as the Yellow Dog River flows through some beautiful rocky terrain. It is around a mile from the wooden bridge crossing to the final falls, and the elevation climbs nearly 175 feet. Along the way, there are a variety of chutes, slides, drops, and cascades. Some of the falls are nearly stacked on top of each other, with just a short, calmer pool between them.

The photo shown to the left is the first major falls you'll come to and the largest of the series. The river makes two big drops here, as well as two sharp turns before continuing downstream.

The final falls of the series are located at: 46° 42.777′ N, 87° 57.193′ W. Here, an island divides the river, and there are two 10-foot sliding falls—one on each side.

Carp River Falls

LOCATION: Near Marquette Mountain

ADDRESS/GPS FOR THE FALLS: 46° 30.241′ N, 87° 26.814′ W

DIRECTIONS: From US-41/M-28 in Marquette, turn south onto McClellan Ave., which becomes Co. Rd. 553. Drive for 2.4 miles, and look for a dirt two-track road leading into the woods on the right. (This is a snowmobile trail in the winter.) Follow this road for 1.3 miles, and there will be a sign for Unnamed Morgan Falls on the left. Drive for 0.2 mile past this point, and look toward the left for a single-track mountain bike trail and a half-buried aqueduct (a very large metal pipe) on the left. Park along the main two-track road, and follow the trail. Unnamed Morgan Falls has a sign reading "This road can be rough, so a high-clearance vehicle is recommended."

WEBSITE: None

WATERWAY: Carp River

HEIGHT: 28 feet **CREST:** 10–30 feet

NEAREST TOWN: Marquette

HIKE DIFFICULTY: Easy to difficult (if you get a close-up look)

TRAIL QUALITY: Good to poor (if you get a close-up look)

ROUND-TRIP DISTANCE: 0.8 mile

ADMISSION: No fee

TRIP REPORT & TIPS:

I have fished the Carp River before, and somehow I'd never been to this beauty. It's a secluded waterfall, with no signs and an indistinct trail. The falls has three drops, beginning with a narrow chute at the top. The river then flattens before cascading over a sprawling rock section and making one more drop at the base.

After parking, follow the single-track biking/hiking trail. This follows the half-buried aqueduct, which eventually becomes fully buried as the trail continues. Stay straight on this trail for 0.3 mile. At this point, look for another trail to the left leading into the woods. Follow this trail, and after 300 feet you get a glimpse of the upper portion of the falls through the trees. Continue on the trail a bit farther, and you'll see the falls from a distance. To get a better look of the falls, as well as get to the base, climb down the steep, muddy, rocky terrain at this point. The photos of the falls in this book were taken by navigating down this tricky terrain. A GPS is recommended to help locate the falls.

Yellow Dog Falls

LOCATION: Big Bay

ADDRESS/GPS FOR THE FALLS: 46° 43.725′ N, 87° 42.382′ W

DIRECTIONS: Starting in Big Bay, drive south on Co. Rd. 550 (Big Bay Rd.) for 1.9 miles, and turn right onto Co. Rd. 510. After another 2.6 miles, turn left to stay on Co. Rd. 510, which is a dirt road from this point on. Stay on this dirt road. Drive for 4 miles, and you'll cross a bridge with small parking areas on the left and along the side of the road. A foot trail then leads into the woods past some boulders.

WEBSITE: None

WATERWAY: Yellow Dog River

HEIGHT: 20 feet **CREST:** 45 feet

NEAREST TOWN: Big Bay

HIKE DIFFICULTY: Fair

TRAIL QUALITY: A good trail, with some creek crossings and rocks near falls

ROUND-TRIP DISTANCE: 1.2 miles

ADMISSION: No fee

TRIP REPORT & TIPS:

From the parking area, hike on the foot trail through a hardwood forest near the winding Yellow Dog River. Along the way you'll need to cross a few small creek beds, which can be a little tricky. Over the years, other visitors have placed logs to help you get across these creeks, but the logs and terrain can be slippery, so watch your footing. Once you reach the falls, your first glimpse is from the top. To get to the base, there are a few different trails that lead down to the bottom. The footing can be slippery, because of the rock and incline, so take your time. At the bottom, the rock extends out into the river, giving you a great look at the falls from below. Here, you can see the river divided by a large rock outcropping and cascading over smaller drops as it meets again just before the base. If you're feeling adventurous, hike downstream along the river for a few smaller waterfalls.

Upper Falls

Lower Falls

Big Garlic Falls

LOCATION: 16 miles northwest of Marquette

ADDRESS/GPS FOR THE FALLS: Upper Falls: 46° 40.051′ N, 87° 37.144′ W;
Lower Falls: 46° 40.041′ N, 87° 37.102′ W

DIRECTIONS: From the intersection of Presque Isle Rd. and Hawley St. on the north side of Marquette, take Hawley St., which then becomes Co. Rd. 550, west and north toward Big Bay for 13.6 miles. Then turn left onto Gold Mine Rd. and follow for 2.8 miles. Turn left onto the two-track road here (between the address markers of N89 and N79), and follow for 200 feet, where it ends. A faint footpath is straight ahead (south) from here.

WEBSITE: None

WATERWAY: Big Garlic River

HEIGHT: Upper Falls: 11 feet; Lower Falls: 12-foot slide and 3-foot drop **CREST:** Varies

NEAREST TOWN: Marquette

HIKE DIFFICULTY: Moderate

TRAIL QUALITY: Fair

ROUND-TRIP DISTANCE: Upper falls: 0.2 mile; distance between upper and lower falls: 0.1 mile

ADMISSION: No fee

TRIP REPORT & TIPS:

The Big Garlic River has quite a few falls as it descends from the hills outside of Marquette toward Lake Superior. Here, I'm covering two of them that are close together and more dramatic in size. From the parking area, follow the faint trail into the woods. The trail will bend right and take you down a hill to the upper falls. The river here makes two drops over the jagged basalt rock, and collects in a small pool before continuing downstream. From here, just follow the river downstream a short ways to see the lower falls.

As you follow the river downstream to the lower falls, the riverbank becomes steep and rocky. This puts you up above the river as it slides through a narrow rocky chute, collects into a pool, and then makes another small drop. To get down to the river (like the photo shows), you'll need to climb down some steep, slippery terrain. Following the trail along this lower falls will lead you to the end of the falls, where the river levels out.

Pinnacle Falls

LOCATION: Yellow Dog Plains

ADDRESS/GPS FOR THE FALLS: 46° 42.374' N, 87° 48.401' W

DIRECTIONS: Starting in Big Bay, drive south on Co. Rd. 550 (Big Bay Rd.) for 1.9 miles, and turn right onto Co. Rd. 510. After another 2.6 miles, you'll pass the turnoff to the left for Co. Rd. 510, but you'll want continue straight on the newly paved AAA Rd. Follow this winding road toward the Yellow Dog Plains for 4.8 miles. Turn left on the major dirt road at this point, which is marked with a yellow Pinnacle Falls Rd. arrow. (Reset your odometer or GPS here.) Drive down this road for 0.5 mile, where you'll pass a trucking/maintenance site on the left and the road will narrow to a two-track road straight ahead. Follow this two-track road. (From this point, there will be side roads and forks, which can make it a bit confusing.) At 1.1 miles, take the left fork, and then at 1.4 miles, take the left fork again. Continue driving, and the two-track road will lead into a recently clear-cut area. At 1.7 miles, turn right onto a two-track road. (During my visit, there was a wooden sign with an arrow at this point.) Then at 2.3 miles, veer left and follow the road to the end at 2.4 miles, where there's a parking area.

WEBSITE: None

WATERWAY: Yellow Dog River

HEIGHT: 16 feet **CREST:** 14 feet

NEAREST TOWN: Big Bay

HIKE DIFFICULTY: Moderate, steep hills, tree roots

TRAIL QUALITY: Fair to poor

ROUND-TRIP DISTANCE: 0.8 mile

ADMISSION: No fee

TRIP REPORT & TIPS:

The drive to this falls is tricky, and the hike there is also somewhat steep. The hike begins on a decent trail through the woods but then quickly degrades when you come to the top of a ridge. The trail heads down this ridge and becomes steep, around a 10 percent grade. This part of the trail also has many washouts with uneven footing. After passing this area, you'll come to a signpost noting the falls; to see them, continue straight past on the trail. The trail head downs another hill, and you'll come to the river. From here, head to the right and follow the worn trail upstream along the river. The trail will end at the falls. Overall, the hike to the falls is a bit of challenge, and the return trip to the parking area is all uphill.

Schweitzer Falls

LOCATION: Palmer

ADDRESS/GPS FOR THE FALLS:
46° 24.432' N, 87° 35.768' W

DIRECTIONS: From Palmer, drive south on M-35 for 0.6 mile, and turn right on Co. Rd. 565. Stay on Co. Rd. 565 for 2.9 miles to a dirt two-track road on the right side of the road. (It is the first dirt road after you cross Schweitzer Creek.) Park along the roadside, and walk the two-track trail.

WEBSITE: None

WATERWAY: Schweitzer Creek

HEIGHT: 21 feet **CREST:** Upper drop 26 feet; lower drop 44 feet

NEAREST TOWN: Palmer

HIKE DIFFICULTY: Fair; narrow trail marked by ribbons

TRAIL QUALITY: Fair; there are fallen trees and some parts are muddy and rocky

ROUND-TRIP DISTANCE: 0.4 mile

ADMISSION: No fee

TRIP REPORT & TIPS:

After parking along the road, start walking the two-track trail for a short distance (117 yards) and look for a slightly wider, cleared area on the right. A hidden trail marked with green ribbons will lead you through the forest to the falls. If you can't find the marked trail, just listen for the falls and start bushwhacking through the trees toward the sound of rushing water. The trail brings you to the base of the falls and to a full view of the lower-level drop. The trail then continues up a ridge next to the falls, and the upper-level drop comes into view, as well as the overall wild, grand display. Having a GPS is helpful.

Warner Falls

LOCATION: Palmer

ADDRESS/GPS FOR THE FALLS:
46° 26.005' N, 87° 35.935' W

DIRECTIONS: From Palmer, drive south on M-35 for 0.7 mile. Look for the waterfall on the right side of the road after a small gas station. It's a little set back and down a bank. A sign along the road also notes its location. For parking, drive to end of the guardrail and park along the shoulder.

WEBSITE: None

WATERWAY: Warner Creek

HEIGHT: 17 feet **CREST:** 3 feet

NEAREST TOWN: Palmer

HIKE DIFFICULTY: Viewable from the road; moderately difficult if you opt for an up-close view

TRAIL QUALITY: Roadside, but steep hill to reach base of waterfall

ROUND-TRIP DISTANCE: Viewable from the road, or 0.2 mile if parking past the guardrail

ADMISSION: No fee

TRIP REPORT & TIPS:

Warner Falls is tucked just enough into the hillside and down a steep bank to make it easy to miss along the road. The best way to see it, though, is on foot, and there are a few different ways to see it other than roadside. The first is marked with a sign saying "Picture Lookout." This short, narrow path leads to an open area with a straight-on view. If you'd like to see the view from the top, another very short trail will lead you there as well. Getting down to the base and pool is manageable, too, but the hillside is very steep and rocky.

Black River Falls

LOCATION: Ishpeming

ADDRESS/GPS FOR THE FALLS:
46° 23.606′ N, 87° 47.164′ W

DIRECTIONS: Starting in downtown Ishpeming, drive south on Co. Rd. 581 (Pine St.) for 9.8 miles, and turn right on Co. Rd. CS. Stay on this dirt road. At 0.6 mile, veer to the right at the fork. Continue for 0.2 mile, and turn right on Co. Rd. CCP. (A wooden sign noting the falls is present here.) Follow this road for 0.4 mile to the end, where there are parking loops. This last stretch often has large puddles, but if you stay to the edge, you can avoid getting stuck.

WEBSITE: None

WATERWAY: Black River

HEIGHT: 27 feet **CREST:** 18 feet

NEAREST TOWN: Ishpeming

HIKE DIFFICULTY: Easy to fair; small hill and rocks to get to base of falls

TRAIL QUALITY: Good; wide dirt path

ROUND-TRIP DISTANCE: 0.4 mile

ADMISSION: No fee

TRIP REPORT & TIPS:

From the parking loop, head north on the wide trail toward the river. After a short ways, you'll reach a very helpful wooden bridge that spans a small ravine. After crossing the bridge, continue on the narrow trail as you pass rock outcroppings. You should be hearing the waterfall at this point, as it's straight ahead. As you approach the falls, use caution with any little trekkers, because you'll be at the top of the waterfall. After taking in the view, follow any number of paths to the right and down a short hill. There will be an angled wooden bridge that gives a decent view of the falls from below.

Unnamed Morgan Falls

LOCATION: Near Marquette Mountain

ADDRESS/GPS FOR THE FALLS: 46° 30.315′ N, 87° 26.271′ W

DIRECTIONS: From US-41/M-28 in Marquette, turn south onto McClellan Ave., which becomes Co. Rd. 553. Drive for 2.4 miles and look for a dirt two-track road leading into the woods on the right. (This is a snowmobile trail in the winter.) Follow this road for just under 1.3 miles, and look for a small parking area and a sign on the left. This road can be rough, so a high-clearance vehicle is recommended.

WEBSITE: None

WATERWAY: Morgan Creek

HEIGHT: 14 feet **CREST:** 15 feet

NEAREST TOWN: Marquette

HIKE DIFFICULTY: Fair

TRAIL QUALITY: Fair, with stairs and a footbridge to the top of falls

ROUND-TRIP DISTANCE: 200 yards

ADMISSION: No fee

TRIP REPORT & TIPS:

The walk to the falls is a short, fun one. First take the wooden staircase down the hillside, and then cross the stream with the help of the wooden bridge. You are now at the top of falls! There is no real trail to the base, so look for the easiest route down the next hill, and your reward is a great view of the falls and the nearby Carp River. If you're a trout fisherman, the Carp River is well known for its trout and salmon fishing.

Big Pup Falls

LOCATION: Big Bay

ADDRESS/GPS FOR THE FALLS:
46° 42.710′ N, 87° 42.238′ W

DIRECTIONS: Starting in Big Bay, drive south on Co. Rd. 550 (Big Bay Rd.) for 1.9 miles, and turn right onto Co. Rd. 510. After another 2.6 miles, turn left to stay on Co. Rd. 510, which is a dirt road from this point on. Stay on this dirt road. After 6.6 miles on Co. Rd. 510, you will cross the Yellow Dog River (see page 72 for Yellow Dog Falls), and then 1.9 miles farther there will be a small creek. That's where you'll want to park roadside for Big Pup Falls. Head left into the woods, before the bridge, to see the falls.

WEBSITE: None

WATERWAY: Big Pup Creek

HEIGHT: 43 feet overall, with drops of 6 feet and 13 feet **CREST:** 6–10 feet

NEAREST TOWN: Big Bay

HIKE DIFFICULTY: Fair

TRAIL QUALITY: Fair

ROUND-TRIP DISTANCE: 350 feet to the base of its cascades; 700 feet overall

ADMISSION: No fee

TRIP REPORT & TIPS:

This waterfall consists of several medium and small cascades, as the creek twists and turns through the rocky terrain. The water here is unbelievably clear, and the setting reminds me of a mountain stream.

After you park along the road, just head across the road and down the bank to reach the falls. A worn footpath follows the stream and will lead you along the cascades and small drops. Since it isn't a maintained trail, expect downed logs and uneven terrain.

Alder Falls

LOCATION: Big Bay

ADDRESS/GPS FOR THE FALLS:
46° 46.924′ N, 87° 42.434′ W

DIRECTIONS: From downtown Marquette, travel northwest out of town on Co. Rd. 550, heading toward Big Bay for 24 miles and take a left on Alder Creek Truck Trail, which isn't marked with a sign. (You'll know you've gone too far on CR-550 if you cross over the Alder Creek bridge.) If that happens, just turn around and head back to the first dirt road on the right. KS Rd. is nearly on the opposite side.) Drive for 0.7 mile on the truck trail and look for a small parking area on the right with a sign stating "No Motorized Vehicles" which references the start of the hiking trail.

WEBSITE: None

WATERWAY: Alder Creek

HEIGHT: 23 feet **CREST:** 10 feet

NEAREST TOWN: Big Bay

HIKE DIFFICULTY: Moderate with steep hill

TRAIL QUALITY: Good; some sand and roots

ROUND-TRIP DISTANCE: 0.2 mile

ADMISSION: No fee

TRIP REPORT & TIPS:

A high-profile vehicle is recommended for this one, as there are washouts. If you're in a car, drive until the road gets rough, park and walk the rest of the way.

The hike to the falls is short but the descent to the creek is fairly steep and sandy, so footing can be tricky. Once you make it to the falls, you are greeted with a view of falls as the water slides down a steep rock face and collects in a pool at the base before continuing downstream.

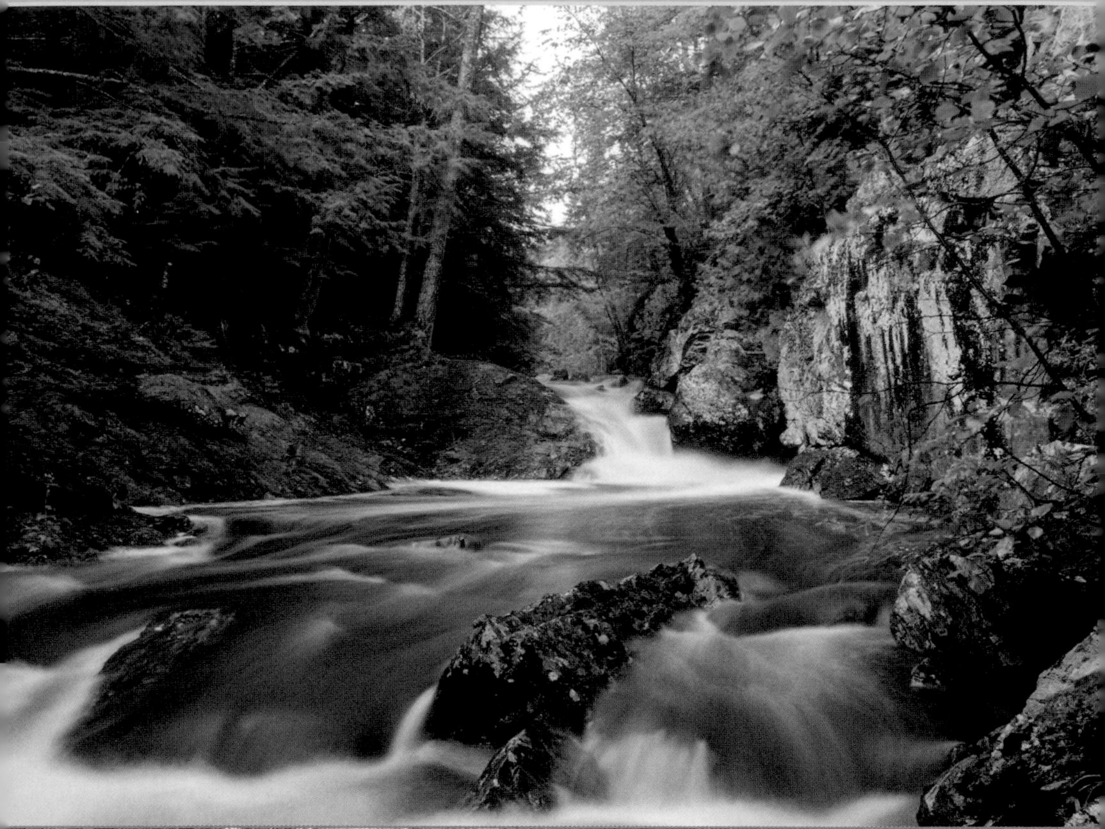

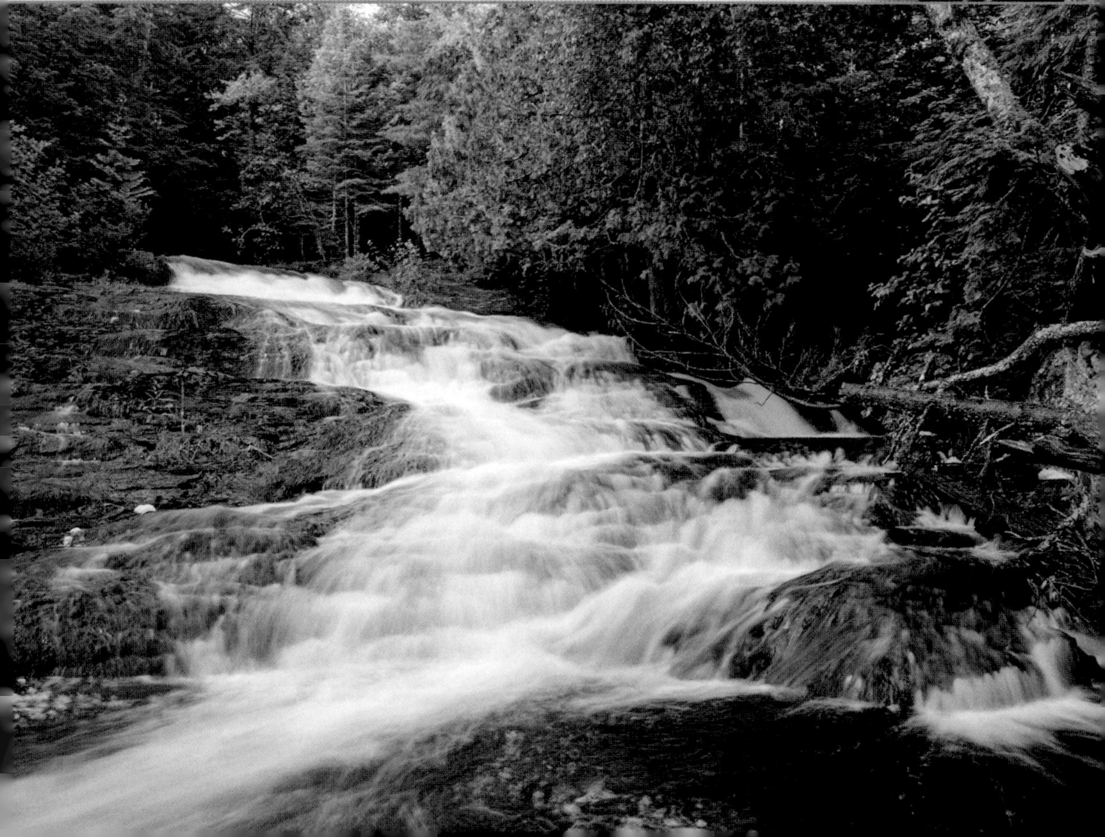

Little Garlic Falls

LOCATION: 12 miles northwest of Marquette

ADDRESS/GPS FOR THE FALLS: 46° 40.010′ N, 87° 34.782′ W

DIRECTIONS: From the intersection of Presque Isle Rd. and Hawley St. on the north side of Marquette, take Hawley St., which then becomes Co. Rd. 550, west and north toward Big Bay for 12 miles. After crossing the Little Garlic River, and just past the parking area for the wilderness area on the left, turn left onto Little Garlic Rd., a dirt road that winds through the woods. Follow for 1.6 miles, and look for a small parking area on the left. After parking, look for a sign across the road for the hiking trail to the falls.

WEBSITE: www.northcountrytrail.org/nct/LittleGarlicFalls.htm

WATERWAY: Little Garlic River

HEIGHT: 12 feet **CREST:** 6–12 feet

NEAREST TOWN: Marquette

HIKE DIFFICULTY: Moderate

TRAIL QUALITY: Fair, with tree roots, rocks, hills

ROUND-TRIP DISTANCE: 2.4 miles

ADMISSION: No fee

TRIP REPORT & TIPS:

The hike to Little Garlic Falls might be better than the waterfall itself. The trail is actually a side spur to the nearby North Country Trail. Along the way, you'll cross small creeks, rock outcroppings, and beautiful forest. Less than a half mile from the falls, there's a MI DNR campsite located along the Little Garlic River.

At the falls, a rock cliff and boulders create a very rugged feel, as the river flows through a narrow rock passage and then slides into a large, deep pool.

Forty Foot Falls

LOCATION: Near Big Bay

ADDRESS/GPS FOR THE FALLS: 46° 49.962′ N, 87° 58.751′ W

DIRECTIONS: From Big Bay, drive south on Co. Rd. 550 (Big Bay Rd.) for 2 miles, then turn right onto Co. Rd. 510 for another 2.6 miles, where you will stay straight to follow the newly paved AAA Rd. Continue another 13 miles (the road turns to dirt after 8 miles, by the nickel-mining operation) to Ford Rd. Turn right on this seasonal road (a high-clearance vehicle is recommended). Drive for 4.3 miles, and veer left onto Northwestern Rd. Drive for 0.7 mile, and turn right onto a two-track trail. Follow for 2.2 miles, and stay on the main road when you come upon side roads. Along the way, you will pass a few hunting camps. The parking is in a cleared opening in the woods, and the falls will be on the right. Bring a GPS for this one.

WEBSITE: None

WATERWAY: Cliff River

HEIGHT: 31 feet **CREST:** 18–36 feet

NEAREST TOWN: Big Bay

HIKE DIFFICULTY: Easy

TRAIL QUALITY: Good

ROUND-TRIP DISTANCE: 340 yards overall; trail heads from parking area to base of falls and back

ADMISSION: No fee

TRIP REPORT & TIPS:

A makeshift campsite is at the top of the falls; it makes for a very short walk, since you can see it from the road. The landscape is rugged, with big boulders and old, giant trees. The top of the falls is relatively open and clear of undergrowth. To get to the base of the falls, just follow one of the trails down along the falls.

Letherby Falls & Upper Letherby Falls

The worn, smooth rock of Letherby Falls & Upper Letherby Falls is some of the most unique I've seen in Michigan.

Upper Letherby Falls

Letherby Falls &
Upper Letherby Falls

Don't miss a visit to nearby Mt. Arvon, Michigan's highest point.

LOCATION: Skanee

ADDRESS/GPS FOR THE FALLS: Letherby Falls: 46° 46.034′ N, 88° 06.521′ W; Upper Letherby Falls: 46° 45.855′ N, 88° 06.492′ W

DIRECTIONS: From Skanee, drive east on Skanee Rd. for 1.5 miles to Roland Lake Rd. and turn right. Heading south, drive for 2.9 miles to the "T." Turn right and you'll now be on Ravine River Rd. (Along the way you'll see signs for Mt. Arvon, as well as orange snowmobile markers for Trail 14, which you're going to want to follow.) Drive for 6.4 miles (you'll spot an unnamed falls along the way) and you'll come to a stop sign. Take a left here. (Turning right will take you to Mt. Arvon). Follow this main road and use the orange Trail 14 signs for guidance. In 1.9 miles you'll come to a fork and keep to the left (Red Jacket Rd. is on the right). From this fork, drive only 0.2 mile, and look for an ATV trail leading into the woods on the left. Park along the road. Then walk down the ATV trail for only 125 yards, and you'll be at the upper falls.

WEBSITE: None

WATERWAY: West Branch Huron River

HEIGHT: Letherby Falls: 14 feet; Upper Letherby Falls: 25 feet **CREST:** Letherby Falls: 18 feet; Upper Letherby Falls: 42 feet

NEAREST TOWN: Skanee

HIKE DIFFICULTY: Fair; small hills

TRAIL QUALITY: Fair; narrow path with rocks and tree roots

ROUND-TRIP DISTANCE: 0.5 mile to see both falls

ADMISSION: No fee

TRIP REPORT & TIPS:

What I love about both Letherby Falls is the very unique carved basalt rock that makes up the waterfalls. Over time, the water has worn away neat channels, round bowls, and rolling, smooth surfaces in each falls. The water is very clear here, and black basalt makes for some really pretty surfaces. Just use caution when walking on it, though, as it is very slippery! What's also nice is that the waterfalls are really close together (350 yards apart), so parking at one and walking to visit both is fairly easy.

The parking area is close to the upper falls. It is also very close to Mt. Arvon (Michigan's highest point), which is a nice destination as well. The gravel roads are suited for car traffic. After parking along the main dirt road, follow the two-track ATV path into the woods and down the hill for 125 yards. You will see the upper falls right away. To get to the main Letherby Falls from here, just follow the river downstream, and you'll approach the falls from above. Navigate your way down and around the rocks to get a better view from the front. Below the main falls, there is also a really nice cascade that's worth checking out.

A really nice cascade just downstream of Letherby Falls

Slate River Falls, Ecstasy Falls, Slide Falls & Kuckuk's Falls

These waterfalls on the Slate River are some of the most challenging and adventurous you'll find in Michigan.

Ecstasy Falls

Slate River Falls, Ecstasy Falls, Slide Falls & Kuckuk's Falls

Set deep within a gorge, the river is your trail for much of this journey to see all of the waterfalls.

LOCATION: Between L'Anse and Skanee

ADDRESS/GPS FOR THE FALLS: Slate River Falls: 46° 49.869′ N, 88° 15.119′ W; Ecstasy Falls: 46° 49.714′ N, 88° 14.899′ W; Slide Falls: 46° 49.646′ N, 88° 14.889′ W; Kuckuk's Falls: 46° 49.584′ N, 88° 14.793′ W

DIRECTIONS: Starting in downtown L'Anse, follow Main St. (which becomes Skanee Rd.), heading north and east toward Skanee. At 11.6 miles, you'll cross over the Slate River Bridge. After about 400 feet, turn right on the next dirt, two-track road. This two-track road can have large puddles, so park off to the side and continue on foot. The two-track road ends, and a footpath leads you from here.

WEBSITE: None

WATERWAY: Slate River

HEIGHT: Slate River Falls: 15 feet; Ecstasy Falls: 18 feet; Slide Falls: 12 feet; Kuckuk's Falls: 10 feet **CREST:** Slate River Falls: 30 feet; Ecstasy Falls: 54 feet; Slide Falls: 48 feet; Kuckuk's Falls: 48 feet

NEAREST TOWN: Skanee

HIKE DIFFICULTY: Moderate to difficult

TRAIL QUALITY: Fair to poor, with no trail in places

ROUND-TRIP DISTANCE: 0.8 miles for just Slate River Falls; 1.9 miles to see all the falls

ADMISSION: No fee

TRIP REPORT & TIPS:

Slate River Falls, as well as the waterfalls beyond it, are an adventure to get to, perhaps more than any waterfalls in Michigan. And that's why I love to visit them! The terrain is tough, rugged, and wild. The falls are situated deep within a steep gorge, and much of the "trail" to the falls is in the river itself. In some spots, climbing up and over the falls is the best option. As you may have guessed, this adds a level of danger based on the river conditions and your physical ability. I highly recommend a GPS for this trek, and when in doubt, don't put yourself at risk.

The first falls of this journey is Slate River Falls (0.4 mile from the parking area). The travel to this one is the easiest of the bunch, but it does require river crossings as you make your way upstream. Based on the time of year, you will need either sandals/water shoes for hot summer days or hip waders when it's not so hot. Along the way, the riverbanks will rise on both sides, and soon you'll notice you're deep in the bottom of a gorge. As you come around the final bend, you're greeted with a great view of the falls and a very large, calm pool.

This is where you can decide to continue farther on to see more waterfalls upstream, or head back. From my experience, once you commit and go onward, there is no turning back or alternate route to get out of the gorge until you're near the final waterfall. Also, if the river is running high and fast at Slate River Falls, then I would recommend *not* going any farther. During my trek, the river was right at the edge of being too much water, and the travel was pretty difficult. It took me about 3 hours to do the round trip. The one bonus is that when you do get near the final waterfall the gorge becomes less steep, and

Slide Falls

Kuckuk's Falls

TRIP REPORT (CONTINUED): you're able to hike up the ridge to a footpath. You can then follow this ridge trail all the way back to the parking area in a short amount of time.

If you want to continue on with the journey, look for a worn path up the left side of Slate River Falls. It's a fairly steep trail up the face of the falls. Once you reach the top, you'll need to re-enter the river and then work your way upstream past rapids and jagged bedrock.

At around 0.7 mile, you reach a really nice, large cascading falls just below the actual Ecstasy Falls, which is only 100 yards farther upstream. Ecstasy Falls is a large, 4-drop falls that resembles very large stair steps. After you navigate up these, the gorge becomes less steep and high. From here you can continue following the river on both land and water to see Slide Falls, which literally looks like a slide. The distance between the top of Ecstasy Falls and Slide Falls is around 125 yards.

From here, continue 0.1 mile farther upstream to the last falls on this journey, Kuckuk's Falls—a wide, steep cascade that flows into a pool before making a sharp bend heading down river. You have reached the final falls!

The quickest route out is to backtrack on the hiking trail and then follow it up along the ridge to the parking area for 0.9 mile.

Canyon Falls

This impressive waterfall is conveniently located at roadside park and makes for a nice spot to stretch your legs while traveling.

During the winter, grab your snowshoes to see the falls

Canyon Falls

Canyon Falls is a great location for autumn colors. I've noticed this area tends to be peak color earlier than other spots.

LOCATION: Canyon Falls Roadside Park, a mile south of Alberta

ADDRESS/GPS FOR THE FALLS: 46° 37.349′ N, 88° 28.598′ W

DIRECTIONS: From Covington, drive north and east on US-141/M-28 for 4 miles, and then, at the T, turn left onto US-41. Drive for 3 miles, and turn into the rest stop on the left. The trail to the waterfall is in the back corner. Here there are pit toilets and picnic tables/grills.

WEBSITE: None

WATERWAY: Sturgeon River

HEIGHT: 15 feet **CREST:** 40 feet

NEAREST TOWN: Covington

HIKE DIFFICULTY: Easy

TRAIL QUALITY: Fair, uneven, and a little muddy in spots

ROUND-TRIP DISTANCE: 0.8 mile

ADMISSION: None

TRIP REPORT & TIPS:

No matter the season, Canyon Falls is a great family stop to enjoy nature and make some memories. It's a fun place to explore the riverbanks, take in a beautiful waterfall, and see an impressive rock canyon that's very unique. On hot summer days, it's not uncommon to see local college kids cliff-jumping at a spot downstream (but don't do this, as it's highly dangerous). Overall, it's just a fun, popular place to easily escape into nature.

The fun begins with a walk down a path that leads directly to the river. Here, you can really take in the wildness of the river and the surrounding landscape. As the walk heads toward the falls, you'll pass some interesting rock features and a few smaller drops on the river. When you reach the falls, you are standing above it, and you get your first taste of the impressive rock canyon. Another viewing area is just a bit downstream, which gives a great perspective of the canyon, with a decent view of it before the river turns to the right. I just love the square-cut rock of the gorge and the lush green ferns that grow nearly anywhere in it. To get a better view of the falls, I like to climb down the rock to the plateau along the river. This gives you a nice side view.

If you want to see more of the canyon as it travels downstream, there is a trail heading north that you will need to look for. Unlike the path to the waterfall, this one is narrower, rockier, and travels along some steep drop-offs. (You'll want to use caution and be extra careful with young children.) It does, however, offer some very scenic perches overlooking the rushing Sturgeon River. After 0.4 mile, the rock canyon levels out, and the river flows down an angled slide to a calmer, wider stretch of river.

Best viewed off-trail on the rock plateau next to the base

Upper Silver Falls

LOCATION: 8 miles southeast of L'Anse

ADDRESS/GPS FOR THE FALLS: 46° 40.816′ N, 88° 19.804′ W

DIRECTIONS: From Herman, drive east on Lystila Rd. for 0.2 mile, and then turn right on Lahti Rd./Summit Rd. Drive for 2 miles (keeping straight at the intersection at 1.8 miles), then turn left onto a two-track road. There is an old gravel pit near this two-track for a landmark. Follow the two-track; don't turn onto any of the side roads you come upon. (This road is bumpy and well worn with some puddles. A high-clearance vehicle is recommended.) At 1.6 miles, look for a side two-track on the right, which is blocked by a small dirt berm a short distance from the road. Park here and continue down this new two-track to see the falls. GPS is highly recommended for the drive and locating the falls.

WEBSITE: None

WATERWAY: Silver River

HEIGHT: 28 feet **CREST:** 9–54 feet

NEAREST TOWN: Herman

HIKE DIFFICULTY: Moderate

TRAIL QUALITY: Fair to poor

ROUND-TRIP DISTANCE: 0.8 mile

ADMISSION: No fee

TRIP REPORT & TIPS:

The trip begins with a walk down the overgrown two-track road. After you enter the woods, the trail becomes narrow and washed out. It's a real ankle-roller, so watch your footing. The trail will eventually lead you to the river, but just before you reach it, there will be a small clearing on the left. Head here and look for a narrower footpath leading into the woods again toward the river. At this point you should also hear the waterfall, so you'll know you're close.

This trail will lead you to the top of the waterfall; it has a really nice upper cascade into a pool with huge boulders. Following the trail, you'll then navigate downstream along the falls, as it twists and turns through more large rocks. At the base, it's hard to get a good view of the falls from top to bottom, so wading to the small rock island will give you a better perspective.

Overall, this is a very nice waterfall with unique features and many drops. To me, the setting feels very old-growth and wild, which I really like.

Black Slate Falls

Quartzite Falls

Black Slate Falls & Quartzite Falls

LOCATION: Between L'Anse and Skanee

ADDRESS/GPS FOR THE FALLS: Black Slate Falls: 46° 47.253′ N, 88° 14.371′ W; Quartzite Falls: N46° 47.329′ W88° 14.508′ W

DIRECTIONS: Starting in downtown L'Anse, follow Main St., which becomes Skanee Rd., to the northeast, toward Skanee. After 11.5 miles, turn right onto Arvon Rd. Head south on this dirt road for 3.4 miles, where there will be a dirt road/snowmobile trail; turn left here. At 0.1 mile there's a bridge over the Slate River. Drive over the bridge and park.

WEBSITE: None

WATERWAY: Slate River

HEIGHT: Black Slate Falls: 7 feet; Quartzite Falls: 15 feet

CREST: Black Slate Falls: 32 feet; Quartzite Falls: 18 feet

NEAREST TOWN: Skanee

HIKE DIFFICULTY: Easy

TRAIL QUALITY: Good

ROUND-TRIP DISTANCE: Black Slate Falls: 180 yards; Quartzite Falls: 315 yards

ADMISSION: No fee

TRIP REPORT & TIPS:

The Slate River features some great waterfalls, and this section of the river features some of the most unique. The slate rock is carved so beautifully here that it almost looks like a staircase. Both of the falls here are easy to reach and close to where you park: Black Slate Falls is upstream and Quartzite Falls is downstream.

To visit Black Slate Falls, follow the river upstream, where a worn path will lead you to the base of the falls. From the base, looking upstream, the falls resembles a grand staircase, as the water flows elegantly over each level.

To see Quartzite Falls, just follow the river downstream from the parking area. The walk is fairly level, and the woods have little underbrush. At the falls, hemlocks line the falls as the river makes a rapid descent through a wide chute of square-cut stone. At the base is a large, calm pool. The stone here is impressive, with near-perfect blocks of slate. In parts, the water slides off the dark stone in a thin curtain of water.

Middle Falls

Lower Falls

Unnamed Falls

Falls River Falls

LOCATION: Downtown L'Anse just off US-41

ADDRESS/GPS FOR THE FALLS: Middle Falls: 46° 45.180′ N, 88° 27.162′ W; Lower Falls: 46° 45.194′ N, 88° 27.200′ W; Unnamed Falls: 46° 45.044′ N, 88° 27.146′ W

DIRECTIONS: Starting in L'Anse near the overhead "Welcome to L'Anse" sign, drive west on US-41 for 0.4 mile. Veer right into a gravel clearing and park. You should see some small signage for the falls. This parking area is just after the Burger King and the railroad tracks that cross the highway.

WEBSITE: None

WATERWAY: Falls River

HEIGHT: Middle Falls: 22 feet; Lower Falls: 10 feet; Unnamed Falls: 7 feet

CREST: Middle Falls: 70 feet; Lower Falls: 30–60 feet; Unnamed Falls: 40 feet

NEAREST TOWN: Downtown L'Anse

HIKE DIFFICULTY: Fair

TRAIL QUALITY: Good, but the trail is a bit uneven and hilly

ROUND-TRIP DISTANCE: Unnamed Falls: 250 yards; Middle Falls/Lower Falls: 0.4 mile

ADMISSION: No fee

TRIP REPORT & TIPS:

Middle & Lower Falls: From the parking area, head to the right (north) and follow the marked trail high up on the bank of the Falls River. Through the trees, you'll see a very long cascading falls to your left. The trail will then veer to the left, and an opening in the trees will give you a great straight-on view of the river, with a railroad bridge at the top of the falls. This long cascade is known as Middle Falls. Continuing on the trail, which is headed downstream and north, you'll see another falls through the trees, not too far from the bench. These are the Lower Falls, which have a unique shape. The left side of the falls has a sharp drop, while the right half is more of a sliding-style cascade. For an unobstructed view, I climbed down the short steep hill to get to the base of the waterfall.

Unnamed Falls: This waterfall is located just over 100 yards from the parking area. You'll need to head to the left (south) and cross the busy US-41 highway. Walk through the ditch, and then cross the railroad tracks, where you should be able to find a trail leading down to the river. The waterfall is straight ahead, upstream. This falls is a traditional drop that spans the entire width of the river.

Middle Silver Falls

Gomanche Falls

Middle Silver Falls & Gomanche Falls

LOCATION: Southeast of L'Anse

ADDRESS/GPS FOR THE FALLS: Middle Silver Falls 1: 46° 45.675′N, 88° 21.667′W; Middle Silver Falls 2: 46° 45.768′N, 88° 21.631′W; Gomanche Falls: 46° 45.635′N, 88° 21.623′W

DIRECTIONS: From L'Anse, drive 0.5 mile south on US-41 to Dynamite Hill Rd. and turn left. Follow it east for 3.6 miles, and then veer left onto Arvon Rd. Drive for 0.6 mile (passing the Silver River bridge along the way), and turn left onto the dirt road, which leads to a gravel pit. Once you enter the gravel pit area, head to the left corner, following the main "trail." The trail will lead back into the woods up a small hill. After a short distance, there will be a "Y" intersection with a less-used two-track leading to the left. (During my visit, there were also the remains of an old bonfire pit.) Park here and walk this left fork, heading northwest. From Arvon Rd. to this spot, it is roughly 0.38 mile.

WEBSITE: None

WATERWAY: Silver River and Gomanche Creek

HEIGHT: Middle Silver Falls 1: 17 feet; Middle Silver Falls 2: 14 feet; Gomanche Falls: 20 feet (full height to Silver River) **CREST:** Middle Silver Falls 1: 40 feet; Middle Silver Falls 2: 40 feet; Gomanche Falls: 15 feet

NEAREST TOWN: L'Anse

HIKE DIFFICULTY: Difficult, steep terrain; some river

TRAIL QUALITY: Poor

ROUND-TRIP DISTANCE: 0.9 mile

ADMISSION: No fee

TRIP REPORT & TIPS:

Start out on the overgrown two-track that eventually ends. Continue heading northwest into the woods, and scramble down the steep hill to the river's edge, which you should hear at this point. I would highly recommend using a GPS. To reach Gomanche Falls, head to the left and follow the river upstream. The waterfall is very visible.

To reach Middle Silver Falls, head downstream from here. You'll encounter some nice cascades after 0.1 mile on your way. To reach the second falls, navigate through the forest downstream for 0.2 mile.

Upper Upper Silver Falls 1

Upper Upper Silver Falls 2

Upper Upper Silver Falls

LOCATION: 7 miles southeast of L'Anse

ADDRESS/GPS FOR THE FALLS: Upper Upper Silver Falls 1: 46° 40.500' N, 88° 19.008' W; Upper Upper Silver Falls 2: 46° 40.585' N, 88° 19.221' W

DIRECTIONS: From Herman, drive east on Lystila Rd. for 0.2 mile, and then turn right on Lahti Rd./Summit Rd. Drive for 2.2 miles (keeping straight east when a road goes south at 1.8 miles and another goes north at 2 miles). At the Y, take the left fork and follow for 0.8 mile to a gated bridge at the Silver River and park. This last stretch of road is rougher and bumpy, so a high-clearance vehicle is recommended.

WEBSITE: None

WATERWAY: Silver River

HEIGHT: Upper Upper Silver Falls 1: 20 feet; Upper Upper Silver Falls 2: 16 feet

CREST: Upper Upper Silver Falls 1: 63 feet; Upper Upper Silver Falls 2: 42 feet

NEAREST TOWN: Herman

HIKE DIFFICULTY: Very difficult, hills and rugged forest

TRAIL QUALITY: No trail; bushwhacking required

ROUND-TRIP DISTANCE: 1.4 miles (0.4 mile to reach 1, then 0.3 mile to reach 2)

ADMISSION: No fee

TRIP REPORT & TIPS:

The Upper Upper Silver Falls are the icing on the cake for waterfalls on the Silver River. During the hike, you'll see a few other nice falls on the river, but I chose to highlight a couple of the biggest and boldest here. The first falls is a very wide, sheer-drop waterfall that resembles a giant rock shelf. The upper portion of this falls is really nice, with a cascade prior to the freefall. The second falls is a fanning, cascade falls.

Because there is no trail to the falls, getting there is difficult. The terrain is hilly, and the underbrush can be thick in spots. With this in mind, I highly recommend using a GPS to find these falls. To reach the falls, you're going to mainly follow the river downstream until you reach the first waterfall. During my travels, I found myself trying to stay on the ridges, as the trees there are bigger and the forest floor was a little clearer. It's about 0.3 mile from the first falls to the second one, and the terrain is very similar along the way. Because of the remoteness and unruly terrain, be sure to bring adequate supplies, just to be safe.

Big Eric's Falls

LOCATION: Big Eric's Bridge State Forest Campground

ADDRESS/GPS FOR THE FALLS: 46° 51.891′ N, 88° 04.962′ W

DIRECTIONS: From Skanee, drive east on Skanee Rd. for 5 miles, until it ends at a three-way stop. Veer right on the dirt road, Big Ericks Rd. Drive for 1.3 miles, where you will cross the bridge and park on the right in a wide clearing along the road.

WEBSITE: None

WATERWAY: Huron River

HEIGHT: 3–5 feet **CREST:** 70 feet

NEAREST TOWN: Skanee

HIKE DIFFICULTY: Fair; narrow trails

TRAIL QUALITY: Good, but trails have rocks and boulders

ROUND-TRIP DISTANCE: 250 yards

ADMISSION: No fee

TRIP REPORT & TIPS:

A popular fishing spot, Big Eric's Falls consist of small drops, cascades, and rapids, as the river flows downstream beneath the bridge and eventually to Lake Superior. Narrow footpaths on both sides of the river will lead you downstream. The flowing river and the old wooden bridge make for some unique photography opportunities.

On a side note, the nearby Big Eric's Bridge State Forest Campground is a quiet, rustic campground overlooking the river from a bluff. This is a really nice spot to enjoy a secluded stay.

Big Falls

LOCATION: Southeast of Big Eric's Bridge State Forest Campground

ADDRESS/GPS FOR THE FALLS: 46° 50.223′ N, 88° 04.410′ W

DIRECTIONS: From Skanee, drive west on Skanee Rd. for 4.7 miles to Black Creek Rd., and turn right (south). Drive for 1.7 miles, and turn left onto a dirt road. Follow for 0.2 mile, and you will reach a river (West Branch Huron River), which you'll need to ford, either on foot or, if you want to risk it, in a vehicle. After crossing the river, take the left fork. Follow for 0.4 mile, where you'll come to another fork. Take the right fork and follow the two-track for 1.5 miles, where there's a small parking area on the left.

WEBSITE: None

WATERWAY: East Branch Huron River

HEIGHT: 17 feet **CREST:** 30 feet each

NEAREST TOWN: Skanee

HIKE DIFFICULTY: Easy to difficult, two-track road with a steep hill to reach base of falls

TRAIL QUALITY: Good to poor, two-track leads to steep hill at falls

ROUND-TRIP DISTANCE: 3.8 miles from river crossing

ADMISSION: No fee

TRIP REPORT & TIPS:

During my visit, the river was running higher than normal and I didn't want to risk getting stuck, so I made the hike to the falls. From the river crossing to the falls, it is all two-track trails. Once you reach the small parking area, you're above the falls. For the best view, you'll want to carefully climb down to the base.

Big Eric's Falls & Big Falls 117

East Branch Falls

LOCATION: East of Big Erick's Bridge

ADDRESS/GPS FOR THE FALLS: 46° 50.959' N, 88° 03.796' W

DIRECTIONS: From the historic Big Erick's Bridge (see Big Eric's Falls, page 116), east of Skanee, drive east on the dirt road (Erick's Rd.) for 1.8 miles. (Along the way you'll come to one fork, at which you should veer right.) You'll cross a small metal bridge, then park on the right in a small clearing. There should also be a small dirt berm ahead of you after parking.

WEBSITE: None

WATERWAY: East Branch Huron River

HEIGHT: 8 feet **CREST:** 36 feet

NEAREST TOWN: Skanee

HIKE DIFFICULTY: Medium

TRAIL QUALITY: Poor; the overgrown two-track trail turns to no trail at all

ROUND-TRIP DISTANCE: 0.8 mile

ADMISSION: No fee

TRIP REPORT & TIPS:

After parking, walk straight ahead, over the small berm, and follow the old two-track trail that's beyond it. The road will eventually dissipate as it continues into woods. From here, follow the GPS coordinates toward the falls. During my travels, I also came across pink ribbons, which lead to the falls. Once you reach the falls, you need to find a way down the steep hill to the river. I ended up going downstream a bit and found a small path to the river.

The falls themselves consist of several cascades curving around a tight bend.

Lower Silver Falls

LOCATION: Northeast of L'Anse

ADDRESS/GPS FOR THE FALLS: 46° 47.566' N, 88° 20.154' W

DIRECTIONS: Starting in downtown L'Anse, follow Main St., which becomes Skanee Rd., northeast toward Skanee. After 7.1 miles, turn right onto Silver Falls Rd. Drive south for 0.6 mile, and turn left at the fork. Follow it to the end, where there's a parking area and a pit toilet.

WEBSITE: None

WATERWAY: Silver River

HEIGHT: Lower section: 14 feet; upper section: 11 feet **CREST:** Lower section: varies; upper section: 5 feet

NEAREST TOWN: L'Anse

HIKE DIFFICULTY: Easy to fair

TRAIL QUALITY: Good

ROUND-TRIP DISTANCE: 0.2 mile

ADMISSION: No fee

TRIP REPORT & TIPS:

Similar to the other falls on the Silver River, Lower Silver Falls features a few different waterfall sections that are located within a short distance. The first, upper cascade is only 125 yards from the parking area. It features a narrow cascade through a jagged ravine of solid rock. Follow the river downstream from here for about 100 yards to see the second section. Here the river is squeezed through a rocky chute and then fans out over a very wide cascade. For the best view of this falls, just follow the river to the pool at the base and look upstream.

Power House Falls

LOCATION: South of L'Anse

ADDRESS/GPS FOR THE FALLS:
46° 44.227′ N, 88° 26.665′ W

DIRECTIONS: From L'Anse, drive south on US-41 for 1.2 miles to Power Dam Rd. and turn right. Follow for 0.7 mile, passing over the railroad tracks, then turn right on the second dirt road. Follow this road to the end, where there's a circle drive. The waterfall is viewable from here.

WEBSITE: None

WATERWAY: Falls River

HEIGHT: 12 feet **CREST:** 35 feet

NEAREST TOWN: L'Anse

HIKE DIFFICULTY: N/A; viewable from the road

TRAIL QUALITY: N/A

ROUND-TRIP DISTANCE: Viewable from the road

ADMISSION: No fee

TRIP REPORT & TIPS:

Power House Falls is a nice, quick side trip if you're passing through the area. The falls is conveniently located close to the parking area, making it accessible for everyone. Next to this nice-looking waterfall is the original powerhouse building, which gives the falls its name. I really like what this old architecture adds to the falls: a visual link to the past.

If you want to see a few other smaller waterfalls close to here, just walk around the building and head upstream for about 150 yards. You'll find three distinct drops, with the biggest being around seven feet tall. These are sometimes referred to as Power Dam Falls.

Ogemaw Falls

LOCATION: Alberta

ADDRESS/GPS FOR THE FALLS:
46° 38.748′ N, 88° 30.443′ W

DIRECTIONS: From L'Anse, take US-41 south for 7.7 miles, and turn right on Baraga Plains Rd. Follow for 1.5 miles, and park along the side of the road on the right. The trail is back up the road a bit and across from a wetland area. A small wooden sign notes the trail to the falls.

WEBSITE: None

WATERWAY: Ogemaw Creek

HEIGHT: 8 feet **CREST:** 6 feet

NEAREST TOWN: L'Anse

HIKE DIFFICULTY: Fair

TRAIL QUALITY: Good

ROUND-TRIP DISTANCE: 250 yards

ADMISSION: No fee

TRIP REPORT & TIPS:

After parking, just walk back up the main road a bit and you'll see a foot trail, with a small wooden sign, on the left (west). This trail will lead you along the creek to the top of falls. Some areas can be muddy. From the top of the falls, it's fairly easy to climb down a very small hill to the base.

As for the falls, it is a small, steep cascade, with very large boulders scattered about. For my photo, I ended up hopping across the creek at a narrow point and photographed from the other side. This waterfall is a nice side visit to the much larger Canyon Falls (page 102), which is just a short drive away.

Agate Falls

The trek to the bottom of Agate Falls is challenging but it features a rewarding view. The many cascades are quite the sight.

View from observation deck

Agate Falls

Don't miss a visit to the top of the overhead steel trestle. The views on each side are definitely worth seeing.

LOCATION: 7 miles southeast of Bruce Crossing

ADDRESS/GPS FOR THE FALLS: 46° 28.848' N, 89° 05.390' W

DIRECTIONS: From Bruce Crossing, drive east on M-28 for 6.9 miles. Turn right into Agate Falls Roadside Park, and follow the loop to the parking spaces.

WEBSITE: www.fs.usda.gov/recarea/ottawa/recarea/?recid=12355

WATERWAY: Middle Branch Ontonagon River

HEIGHT: 42 feet **CREST:** 95 feet

NEAREST TOWN: Trout Creek

HIKE DIFFICULTY: Easy to difficult

TRAIL QUALITY: Good to poor; an observation deck/paved path leads to steep, narrow terrain

ROUND-TRIP DISTANCE: 0.4 mile from parking area to viewing platform; 0.5 mile from parking area to base of falls

ADMISSION: No fee

TRIP REPORT & TIPS:

Overall, Agate Falls is impressive in size and beauty. An old steel railroad trestle (now used for a snowmobile/ORV trail) spans the falls, adding to the scenery. The falls are also conveniently located near a roadside park, making it a great stop for stretching your legs after a long drive or for a picnic lunch.

A nice paved path will get you to the falls; the path follows the river downstream, under the highway's bridge, and then to a wooden walkway and observation deck. The view from the deck offers a glimpse of the falls and a forested valley farther downstream. There are actually two other views of the falls, but they require tackling some steep terrain on "unofficial" trails.

The first unique view is at the base of the falls. To get there, you're going to have to climb down some narrow, steep trails beyond the wooden observation deck. I like to call these "billy-goat trails," as they are narrow trails traversing the hillside. Once you reach the base, you are greeted with a straight-on view of the falls and a picturesque cascade. I really like the old railroad trestle spanning above the falls, as it adds in an element of local history.

This leads me into the second unique view you need to see while visiting Agate Falls: the overhead view from atop the spanning railroad trestle. Here you're greeted with picturesque scenery on both sides of the trestle and an awesome overhead view of the falls! To get up there, start from the parking loop on the north side of the road. There you'll find two trails that head to the snowmobile trail over the bridge.

The old steel railroad trestle can be seen here spanning the falls

Bond Falls

Bond Falls might be one of the most under-appreciated waterfalls in Michigan. An upstream dam provides constant flow throughout the year.

Bond Falls

Plan to spend some time here as there are variety of great viewing areas from top to bottom.

LOCATION: Bond Falls Scenic Site

ADDRESS/GPS FOR THE FALLS: 46° 24.609′ N, 89° 07.992′ W

DIRECTIONS: From Watersmeet, drive north on US-45 for 10 miles, and turn right on Bond Falls Rd. Drive for 3.1 miles, and look for a sign and a driveway on the left. (If you continue 0.2 mile farther on Bond Falls Rd., you will come to a picnic area I suggest for winter parking.) If coming from Bruce Crossing, drive south on US-45 for 9.2 miles, and turn left on Bond Falls Rd.

WEBSITE: www.michigandnr.com/parksandtrails/Details.aspx?id=412&type=SPRK

WATERWAY: Middle Branch Ontonagon River

HEIGHT: 51 feet **CREST:** 48–190 feet

NEAREST TOWN: Paulding

HIKE DIFFICULTY: Good to moderate; there are stairs for upper falls

TRAIL QUALITY: Good to fair, paved and wooden path; narrow, steep for upper falls

ROUND-TRIP DISTANCE: 0.2 mile

ADMISSION: Michigan Recreation Passport required (see page 12)

TRIP REPORT & TIPS:

Because of its remote location in the western Upper Peninsula, Bond Falls doesn't get a lot of attention, but it is definitely a must-see in my book. To me, it's right up there with Upper Tahquamenon Falls in beauty and "wow" factor.

Overall, it is a very large, steep cascade, with the rock angling out from the hillside. A convenient barrier-free boardwalk gives you multiple angles from both sides of the falls. The falls are accessible to anyone, thanks to the paved walk that starts from the parking area and leads through the woods. One of my favorite things is hearing the falls before you see it. These falls are loud!

After viewing the falls from the bottom, make sure to follow the path to the right into the woods for another section of the falls upstream. Getting here can be challenging, due to the steep terrain and stairs, but the trail follows up along Bond Falls and offers some great views from midway up. Continuing up along the falls to the top and beyond, you'll come to a smaller section of waterfalls that is unique. The way the water flows so smoothly over the rock is truly beautiful.

I also recommend making a winter visit here. Unlike many waterfalls, this one doesn't freeze over. The state park's parking lot isn't plowed during the winter, so you're going to want to park along the main road and then walk downstream to get to the base of the falls.

The view from the trail that follows the falls upstream

O Kun de Kun Falls
& Peanut Butter Falls

O Kun de Kun Falls is a remote and wild waterfall along the well-known North Country National Scenic Trail.

Peanut Butter Falls

O Kun de Kun Falls & Peanut Butter Falls

Don't confuse the smaller, upstream Peanut Butter Falls with O Kun de Kun Falls. Keep following the trail a short distance. The sight of the large wooden suspension bridge is a sign you've arrived.

LOCATION: Ottawa National Forest

ADDRESS/GPS FOR THE FALLS: O Kun de Kun Falls 46° 39.075′ N, 89° 09.144′ W; Peanut Butter Falls: 46° 39.009′ N, 89° 09.306′ W

DIRECTIONS: From Bruce Crossing, drive north on US-45 for 8.3 miles. Turn right into parking lot for the trailhead for the falls.

WEBSITE: www.fs.usda.gov/ottawa

WATERWAY: Baltimore River

HEIGHT: O Kun de Kun Falls: 26 feet; Peanut Butter Falls: 10 feet

CREST: O Kun de Kun Falls: 42–68 feet; Peanut Butter Falls: 60–75 feet

NEAREST TOWN: Bruce Crossing

HIKE DIFFICULTY: Moderate; there are small hills, and it can be slippery

TRAIL QUALITY: Fair to poor

ROUND-TRIP DISTANCE: 2.8 miles

ADMISSION: No fee

TRIP REPORT & TIPS:

O Kun de Kun Falls is another waterfall that I knew very little about before seeing it for myself. I had seen a few photos, but that's about it. Compared to some of the other larger ones in the area, like Bond Falls and Agate Falls, this one is off the beaten path, but that's part of the fun. Overall, it's impressive in size, and its water drops straight down, something that's pretty unusual. For an interesting perspective, there is a hollow space behind the waterfall where you can get a view from behind the falling water!

It takes a lengthy hike to get to the falls. It starts with a gravel path and narrow wood planks, but that all disappears after a short distance. After that, I found the mixed-clay trail to be very muddy and slick. Along the trail, the forest is very thick, so you're essentially forced to walk on the trail. On my hike, I came across bear tracks and scat in the mud, so my head was on a swivel! Unfortunately, I didn't encounter any furry friends.

Along the way, and upstream of O Kun de Kun Falls, there is a smaller waterfall that's worth checking out, called Peanut Butter Falls. At 1.2 miles in, there is a side trail that heads down a steep trail, with the waterfall at the bottom. From there, hike back up the hill and continue to the right to reach the main attraction, which is only 0.2 mile away.

You'll approach the falls from the top, where you'll get a great panoramic view of the waterfall. Farther downstream there is a large wooden footbridge spanning the river. To get to the base of the falls, there are some side trails that navigate to a large rock outcropping, where you can get a pretty good idea just how big this falls really is.

If you continue following the main trail downstream, it will lead to and across the very large wooden bridge. After crossing the bridge, I headed to the right and followed some smaller trails upstream to the falls again, this time on the opposite side. If you venture here, check out the giant rock slabs and the thick woods.

Upper Falls

Middle Falls

Lower Falls

Duppy Falls

LOCATION: Ottawa National Forest

ADDRESS/GPS FOR THE FALLS: Falls 1: 46° 24.796′ N, 88° 54.668′ W; Falls 2: 46° 24.768′ N, 88° 54.667′ W; Falls 3: 46° 24.744′ N, 88° 54.667′ W

DIRECTIONS: Starting in Kenton on Highway M-28, drive south for 5.2 miles on NF-16. Turn right onto Forest Service Road 3645, which is a narrow, dirt, two-track road. (This will be the second of 2 two-track roads next to each other.) Drive for 0.2 mile to a large clearing and park. This road is bumpy and washed out in parts, so you may want to park at the road entrance and hike in.

WEBSITE: www.fs.usda.gov/ottawa

WATERWAY: Jumbo River

HEIGHT: Falls 1: 9 feet; falls 2: 12 feet; falls 3: 11 feet **CREST:** Falls 1: 30 feet; falls 2: 5–27 feet; falls 3: 27 feet

NEAREST TOWN: Kenton

HIKE DIFFICULTY: Fair

TRAIL QUALITY: Fair; some slippery rock and small hills

ROUND-TRIP DISTANCE: 0.8 mile (to see all 3 falls)

ADMISSION: No fee

TRIP REPORT & TIPS:

After parking in the clearing, look west for a narrow hiking path leading into the woods. Follow this for a short distance to reach the narrow State Creek and a small footbridge. Continue on the trail, and you'll then reach the Jumbo River. The footpath follows the river until you reach the first waterfall, a split, dropping falls. The moss-covered slate rocks here can be slippery, so watch your footing. Continue on the path up along the falls to reach the second waterfall, which is only 130 yards upstream. This one is a little grander, with a nice swirling bend and several drops. The final falls is just 80 yards farther upstream and features a nice sliding falls with a large pool.

View from along the river's edge

The main walking path passes this great view of the river and Misicot Falls

Misicot Falls *(Piers Gorge)*

LOCATION: Piers Gorge Scenic Area

ADDRESS/GPS FOR THE FALLS: 45° 45.488′ N, 87° 56.939′ W

DIRECTIONS: From the town of Norway, head south on US-8 for 2 miles, and turn right onto Piers Gorge Rd. Drive 3.1 miles to the parking area at the end. A Michigan DNR sign noting Piers Gorge greets you.

WEBSITE: None

WATERWAY: Menominee River

HEIGHT: 8 feet **CREST:** 130 feet

NEAREST TOWN: Norway

HIKE DIFFICULTY: Fair

TRAIL QUALITY: Fair, with rocks, small hills, and tree roots

ROUND-TRIP DISTANCE: Misicot Falls (pier 3): 0.8 mile; pier 4: 2.6 miles

ADMISSION: Michigan Recreation Passport required (see page 12)

TRIP REPORT & TIPS:

Piers Gorge might be one of the finest hidden gems in the Upper Peninsula of Michigan. This wild and scenic stretch of river on the Menominee River (the border between Michigan and Wisconsin) is a great place to spend some time exploring and witnessing the raw power of water. The main feature here are four piers; each pier is a set of rapids and drops within the gorge. Piers one through three are located relatively close together; this is my favorite stretch of the river. The fourth pier is quite a hike beyond the others and the least appealing.

Pier number three is where you'll find Misicot Falls, which is a distinguished drop on the very wide river. Below this falls, the river becomes very wild, with all sorts of whitewater activity. I mention whitewater because this gorge is said to offer some of the best whitewater rafting in the Midwest. Local outfitters offer rafting trips, so you can give it a try yourself. If you visit during the spring melt, expect to see some world-class athletes paddling the raging river.

To see the piers, just follow the main path from the parking area. As you walk the path, wooden posts help distinguish where the separate piers are located. If you're the type to adventure off the trail, like me, there are several smaller side trails that travel along the river and over some really neat rock formations that are almost prehistoric-looking.

Jumbo Falls

LOCATION: South of Kenton, Ottawa National Forest

ADDRESS/GPS FOR THE FALLS: 46° 26.976′ N, 88° 54.778′ W

DIRECTIONS: From Kenton, drive west on M-28 for 1.7 miles, then turn left on Golden Glow Rd. Follow for 1.6 miles, and take another left on Jumbo Pit Rd. Drive for 0.3 mile and veer right. After 0.7 mile you will reach an old gravel pit; continue through it for close to 0.3 mile to the end. A small parking area and signage will greet you.

WEBSITE: www.fs.usda.gov/main/ottawa

WATERWAY: Jumbo River

HEIGHT: 8 feet **CREST:** 15 feet

NEAREST TOWN: Kenton

HIKE DIFFICULTY: Easy

TRAIL QUALITY: Good

ROUND-TRIP DISTANCE: 275 yards

ADMISSION: No fee

TRIP REPORT & TIPS:

Jumbo Falls is an easy falls to reach, as its nice, short trail winds through hemlocks and cedars. The falls is a wide cascade made up of crystal-clear water flowing over black slate rock. Below the falls, the water collects into a large pool before continuing on downstream. While there, I tried doing some trout fishing but didn't have any luck. The river, though, has a number of bends that looked like a perfect place for a trout or two to be hiding.

Victoria Dam Falls

LOCATION: Rockland

ADDRESS/GPS FOR THE FALLS: 46° 41.229′ N, 89° 13.758′ W

DIRECTIONS: From US-45 in Rockland, head west on Elm Rd., which becomes Victoria Dam Rd. Follow this hilly, winding road for 4.8 miles. When you reach the dam area, there will be a fork. The right fork will take you to a view of the reservoir and boat launch. The left fork will take you closer to the dam viewing area. Follow the left fork until it ends; you'll see the gated road.

WEBSITE: None

WATERWAY: West Branch Ontonagon River

HEIGHT: 72 feet **CREST:** 128 feet

NEAREST TOWN: Rockland

HIKE DIFFICULTY: Easy

TRAIL QUALITY: Good

ROUND-TRIP DISTANCE: 0.2 mile

ADMISSION: No fee

TRIP REPORT & TIPS:

These falls are a byproduct of the Victoria Dam and controlled by the radial arm floodgates up on the dam. The power company releases excess water (creating the falls) when the reservoir exceeds capacity. The best time to see the falls is during the spring melt and into the early summer. At other times, there may be nothing at all, so this is completely based on the seasons and conditions.

To see the falls, just continue walking past the gate and follow the service road to the right. This will take you near the base of the dam and just across from the falls.

Ajibikoka Falls

LOCATION: Ottawa National Forest

ADDRESS/GPS FOR THE FALLS:
46° 19.804′ N, 89° 14.252′ W

DIRECTIONS: From Watersmeet, drive north on US-45 for 3.1 miles. Turn left onto Sucker Lake Rd., a dirt road, and drive west for 3.6 miles. On the right will be Forest Road 5120, which is marked with a plastic marker and is an ATV-only road. It is gated a short distance from the main road; park near here.

WEBSITE: www.fs.usda.gov/recarea/ottawa/recarea/?recid=12349

WATERWAY: Sucker Creek

HEIGHT: 13 feet (main drop at base)

CREST: 3–6 feet

NEAREST TOWN: Watersmeet

HIKE DIFFICULTY: Moderate

TRAIL QUALITY: Fair to poor

ROUND-TRIP DISTANCE: 1.4 miles

ADMISSION: No fee

TRIP REPORT & TIPS:

For those looking for a little adventure, this is one waterfall to visit. It's quite a trek to get to these unique falls, which resemble a natural dam of sorts.

Begin heading northeast on Forest Road 5120, a two-track, ATV-only road. The trail is narrow and overgrown but distinct enough to follow. At about 0.5 mile, on your right, you'll see an old logging road veering to the northeast. More a clearing than a road, it's easier than bushwhacking. From this spot, you're 0.2 mile from the falls. If you follow the clearing you'll hear the falls and can follow the sound. Or use a GPS to hone in on the coordinates.

Mex-i-min-e Falls

LOCATION: 7 miles northeast of Watersmeet

ADDRESS/GPS FOR THE FALLS: 46° 18.806′ N, 89° 03.241′ W

DIRECTIONS: From Watersmeet, head north on US-45 a short ways, and turn right on Old U.S. Hwy 2. Drive for 6.5 miles, and then turn left on Forest Road 4500. Follow this dirt road for 1.1 miles, and then turn left into the Burned Dam Campground. Park in the day-use area, and walk to the river and falls to the west.

WEBSITE: www.fs.usda.gov/recarea/ottawa/recarea/?recid=12352

WATERWAY: Middle Branch Ontonagon River

HEIGHT: 8 feet **CREST:** 20 feet

NEAREST TOWN: Watersmeet

HIKE DIFFICULTY: Easy

TRAIL QUALITY: Good

ROUND-TRIP DISTANCE: 300 feet

ADMISSION: No fee

TRIP REPORT & TIPS:

If you're looking for a nice quiet spot in the Ottawa National Forest, especially for camping, visit Mex-i-min-e Falls. The waterfall is conveniently located within the Burned Dam Campground and is just a short walk from the campsites and parking. This small cascading falls is created by the wide river flowing through a narrowing rock outcropping. Downstream, the river widens again and also makes for some nice canoeing or kayaking. The history of the area is interesting, too. During the logging era, this area was the site of a dam, which was later destroyed in forest fires.

Ajibikoka Falls & Mex-i-min-e Falls 141

Chicagon Falls

LOCATION: Crystal Falls Township

ADDRESS/GPS FOR THE FALLS: 46° 08.053′ N, 88° 27.176′ W

DIRECTIONS: From Crystal Falls, drive west on US-2 for 5.1 miles to Long Lake Rd. Turn right, and continue for 3.1 miles to a two-track road on the right. This road is marked only with a sign reading "Raymers." (Digital mapping software labels it as Dave's Camp Rd.) Drive for 0.2 mile to a road on the right. There will be a sign saying "Raymers," as well as a "Falls" sign. This new road gets rougher as you follow the signs, so park where you feel comfortable, depending on the type of vehicle you're driving. A car/van can drive on for 0.4 mile and park near the driveway for "Raymers." Beyond here the road becomes washed out and sandy. A high-clearance vehicle with four-wheel drive could possibly make it all the way to the falls.

WEBSITE: None

WATERWAY: Chicagon Slough

HEIGHT: 14 feet **CREST:** 18 feet

NEAREST TOWN: Crystal Falls

HIKE DIFFICULTY: Fair

TRAIL QUALITY: Fair, two-track trail, with some rocks at the falls

ROUND-TRIP DISTANCE: 1.8 miles from the first parking option and back

ADMISSION: No fee

TRIP REPORT & TIPS:

The hike to this falls isn't bad; you'll head through the woods and to a clear-cut area. As you approach, listen for the sound of rushing water and look for the loop parking area. A short footpath leads you into the forest and to the top of the falls.

Fumee Falls

LOCATION: Roadside park east of Iron Mountain

ADDRESS/GPS FOR THE FALLS: Rest stop along US-2, Quinnesec / 45° 48.377′ N, 87° 58.706′ W

DIRECTIONS: From Iron Mountain, drive east on US-2 for 4.8 miles, and the waterfall will be on the left (north) side of the road. This area is a pull-off rest stop.

WEBSITE: None

WATERWAY: Fumee Creek

HEIGHT: 16 feet (upper level has two drops that total 14 feet) **CREST:** 18 feet

NEAREST TOWN: Quinnesec

HIKE DIFFICULTY: Easy

TRAIL QUALITY: Maintained path, with staircase and overlook

ROUND-TRIP DISTANCE: Viewable from road

ADMISSION: No fee

TRIP REPORT & TIPS:

Fumee Falls is located just east of Iron Mountain, on US-2, and is part of a nice little roadside park. This waterfall is quite accessible, as it's located along the road, and there are nicely paved paths. Next to the falls, there is a large staircase, which leads you to a viewing platform at the top. From there, you get a nice overhead perspective of the falls, as well as an additional upper set of falls. Like many waterfalls, this one can be nearly dry during rainless summers.

Superior Falls

Superior Falls is a beautiful, rugged waterfall deep within a rocky gorge that divides the states of Michigan and Wisconsin.

The easy-to-reach top view

Superior Falls

*Because of its out-the-way location, Superior Falls tends to fly under radar.
I highly recommend adding it to your list.*

LOCATION: Michigan/Wisconsin border near Lake Superior

ADDRESS/GPS FOR THE FALLS: East 230 Lake Rd., Ironwood, MI / Top view:
46° 33.823′ N, 90° 24.905′ W; Bottom view: 46° 33.805′ N, 90° 24.944′ W

DIRECTIONS: Starting in Ironwood, drive west on US-2 into Wisconsin for 11 miles.
Turn right (north) on Hwy. 122. After 4.2 miles, you will cross the Montreal River and
be back in Michigan. Continue another 0.5 mile, and turn left onto the dirt road that
has a sign noting the falls. Follow this dirt road to the end, where there's a parking lot.

WEBSITE: None

WATERWAY: Montreal River

HEIGHT: 45 feet (main falls) **CREST:** 25 feet

NEAREST TOWN: Ironwood

HIKE DIFFICULTY: Top view: Easy; Bottom view: Difficult

TRAIL QUALITY: Good to fair

ROUND-TRIP DISTANCE: Top view: 325 yards; Bottom view: 0.8 mile

ADMISSION: No fee

TRIP REPORT & TIPS:

Superior Falls lives up to its name. It's an impressive waterfall on the Montreal River. Similar to the upstream Saxon Falls (page 148), it is found deep within a rocky gorge, just before the river flows into Lake Superior. Along the way, the river flows over a variety of rocky drops and cascades, before making its final plunge at Superior Falls into a very large pool.

To see the falls, there are two different viewing options, and each offers a different perspective. The view from the top is easy to access and lets you get a look from high above the falls. The view from the bottom is more difficult to reach but provides a unique experience deep within the gorge. If you're physically able to do both, I recommend it!

For the top view, head to the left after parking and past the fenced-in power station structures (signs on the fence help give direction). A short trail will lead into the woods and follow a fence line. The fence does obstruct the view, but there's a point near the end where you can get a clear view of the falls and the rocky terrain upstream. To view the falls from below, head to the right after parking. The most difficult part about this trek to the base of the waterfall is a steep paved path that leads down to the river and Lake Superior. (The walk down isn't difficult; it's the hike back up that can be tiring.) Once you do reach the river mouth, head to the left and walk upstream toward the falls. You'll pass by a power company building. I found this part to be really fun and adventurous. The cliff walls rise up on both sides of the river, and the waterfall is hidden from view until the last second. When you get there, it's hard to believe this is still Michigan or the Midwest! On your way back, before the steep hill, don't miss a visit to Lake Superior.

Saxon Falls

Saxon Falls is another waterfall that doesn't get a lot of attention but it is absolutely gorgeous and worth the extra drive.

Saxon Falls

Saxon Falls is the only waterfall in this guide where your vehicle will be parked in a different state!

LOCATION: Michigan/Wisconsin border near Lake Superior

ADDRESS/GPS FOR THE FALLS: 46° 32.142′ N, 90° 22.705′ W

DIRECTIONS: Starting in Ironwood, drive west on US-2 into Wisconsin for 9.5 miles. Turn right on Co. Rd. B. At 2.4 miles, the road will turn to the left, but you'll want to continue straight on Saxon Falls Rd. After 0.4 mile, take the road to the right, and continue for another 0.6 mile to a parking area. The last mile is well marked with signs. (Don't miss visiting nearby Superior Falls before or after this visit.)

WEBSITE: None

WATERWAY: Montreal River

HEIGHT: 84 feet **CREST:** Varies

NEAREST TOWN: Ironwood

HIKE DIFFICULTY: Fair, but potentially dangerous cliffs

TRAIL QUALITY: Good

ROUND-TRIP DISTANCE: 1.2 miles

ADMISSION: No fee

TRIP REPORT & TIPS:

I found Saxon Falls to be a fun waterfall to visit, as the trek starts in Wisconsin but then crosses over to the Michigan side for viewing. Similar to Superior Falls (page 144) downstream, this is another large waterfall worth checking out. The Montreal River descends over two big plunges and into a deep gorge.

After parking, head left toward the river, where you'll see the metal penstock for the dam, with a catwalk on top. Climb atop and head to the left to cross over the river on the catwalk. (You're now in Michigan!) Continue on the catwalk until you reach the fenced-off portion. Here, you'll want to take the left stairway into the woods. (The option to the right is no longer used.) The decent hiking path will take you to the top of Saxon Falls. From here, the trail continues along the edge of the deep gorge to another viewing spot with scenic views in both directions. There are no barriers keeping you from the edge of the cliff, and the footing can be loose, so use extra caution. Continuing on, there is one more vantage point, which offers a great perspective of the waterfall in its entirety and the gorge to your back.

The convenient catwalk crossing the Montreal River, which is also the state line

Saxon Falls 151

Gabbro Falls

Located on the scenic Black River, Gabbro Falls is the hidden gem on this already impressive river.

This double-plunging falls has a thunderous roar during the wet seasons

Gabbro Falls

Make sure to grab hold of your little ones here. There are no railings and the viewing spot is high above the river.

LOCATION: Bessemer, near Blackjack Ski Resort

ADDRESS/GPS FOR THE FALLS: 46° 30.129′ N, 89° 59.569′ W

DIRECTIONS: Starting in Bessemer, head east on US-2 for 3 miles. Turn left onto Blackjack Rd. and follow it. At 1.6 miles, veer left and continue on Blackjack Rd., heading toward Blackjack Ski Resort. After crossing a wooden bridge, turn left and continue on Blackjack Rd., now a dirt road. After 0.3 mile, there will be yellow gates and old buildings on the right. Park here along the shoulder, and walk across the road to the east looking for a trail into the woods.

WEBSITE: None

WATERWAY: Black River

HEIGHT: 53 feet **CREST:** 50 feet

NEAREST TOWN: Bessemer

HIKE DIFFICULTY: Easy

TRAIL QUALITY: Fair, but narrow and with cliffs

ROUND-TRIP DISTANCE: 500 feet

ADMISSION: No fee

TRIP REPORT & TIPS:

Also known as Baker Falls, this wild and rugged waterfall doesn't get a lot of attention like the other waterfalls farther downstream on the Black River. Overall, this one is large, with big plunges and a unique shape. It features multiple, large drops and is divided by a rock cliff that forms two separate falls. What's also unique is the vantage point. You are standing across from the falls on an adjacent rock cliff; please take serious caution! The rock surface can be slippery, and there are no railings to prevent an accident. During higher water levels, the mist and wind generated by the crashing water is incredible.

To reach the falls after parking, just look for a narrow footpath leading into the woods. The distance from the road to viewing is very short. During my visit, there were some college kids adventuring to the base of the falls, which is possible, albeit very challenging, as the descent is steep and muddy. To me, it didn't look like it was worth the effort.

Little Trap Falls

LOCATION: White Pine

ADDRESS/GPS FOR THE FALLS: 46° 41.387′ N, 89° 33.383′ W

DIRECTIONS: From Bergland, drive north on M-64 for 9.6 miles. Turn right on Old M-64, a seasonal, dirt road. Head south for 2.1 miles, and park along the road.

WEBSITE: None

WATERWAY: Anderson Creek

HEIGHT: 27 feet   **CREST:** 1–10 feet

NEAREST TOWN: White Pine

HIKE DIFFICULTY: Difficult

TRAIL QUALITY: No trail, GPS required

ROUND-TRIP DISTANCE: 0.2 mile

ADMISSION: No fee

TRIP REPORT & TIPS:

It takes a little bit of work to find and access this waterfall, but you're well rewarded when you get there. Located only a short distance from the nearby road, there is no trail and the creek is small, so there aren't many indications that a waterfall this tall is there until you come up right on it.

With a GPS, I would first set a waypoint for the falls and then head east toward those coordinates from the road. The forest itself is fairly easy to navigate, except for two steep ravines you'll pass through before approaching the falls from downstream. As you walk the short distance upstream, the canyon walls will grow taller (over 40 feet), and the falls will be the prize at the end of this narrow gorge.

This can be a seasonal waterfall, so visits in the spring and early summer are best, as well as after a rainfall.

Yondota Falls

LOCATION: 3 miles north of Marenisco, Ottawa National Forest

ADDRESS/GPS FOR THE FALLS: 46° 25.820' N, 89° 41.084' W

DIRECTIONS: From Marensico at US-2, drive north on Co. Rd. 523. After passing over the Presque Isle River bridge, 3.3 miles from US-2, park along the road on the wide shoulder. A sign and hiking trail are on the left.

WEBSITE: www.fs.usda.gov/recarea/ottawa/recarea/?recid=12345

WATERWAY: Presque Isle River

HEIGHT: 16 feet (first plunge) **CREST:** Varies

NEAREST TOWN: Marenisco

HIKE DIFFICULTY: Moderate

TRAIL QUALITY: Poor, rocky surface and tree roots

ROUND-TRIP DISTANCE: 0.4 mile

ADMISSION: No fee

TRIP REPORT & TIPS:

After parking, follow the narrow trail into the woods, which is also marked with a small sign. The trail is narrow and rocky in parts. Look for a trail veering to the left to view the start of Yondota Falls. The river here is squeezed through the basalt rock outcropping and makes a nice plunge. From here, the water cascades over more rocks and boulders, as the elevation drops about 50 feet over a 400-foot stretch of river. At the base, the river collects in a large, calm pool before continuing downstream.

After viewing the upper drop, backtrack to the main trail and continue west to see the long cascade and pool area.

Judson Falls

LOCATION: South of Lake Gogebic

ADDRESS/GPS FOR THE FALLS: 46° 23.382' N, 89° 33.680' W

DIRECTIONS: From Marenisco, drive east on US-2 for 9.5 miles to Stage Coach Rd. Turn left (north) and drive for 2.8 miles to the unmarked two-track on the left.

WEBSITE: None

WATERWAY: Slate River

HEIGHT: 12 feet **CREST:** 25 feet

NEAREST TOWN: Marenisco

HIKE DIFFICULTY: Fair

TRAIL QUALITY: Fair, two-track and some mud

ROUND-TRIP DISTANCE: 4 miles (from main road)

ADMISSION: No fee

TRIP REPORT & TIPS:

The hike to the falls isn't difficult, as it mostly consists of two-track roads, but the distance you'll need to hike depends largely on the type of vehicle you're driving and the road conditions. If you're in a car or van, park along Stage Coach Rd. and hike in. A higher-clearance vehicle and four-wheel drive could make it farther in, so park where you're comfortable, and hike the rest of the way. Overall, the trail looks to be mainly used by ATVs. Having a GPS will also help get you in and out.

As for the path, there are only a few turns, and you're staying on the main, heavily used trail. There are areas where the road splits, but those tend to be overgrown. One notable landmark is an orange gate at around 0.9 mile in. Here you'll just want to continue on the main two-track to the right. As you get closer to the falls, the trail will lead into a darker, wet forest of cedars. At 1.9 miles you are very close to the river and falls. The sound of rushing water is audible this point, and a rough path will break off the main trail to the left. Follow this path to the river, and then start heading downstream from here, as you are very close to the top of the falls!

On the hot summer day I visited, the falls were a perfect place to cool down after the hike. The old cedar forest provided much-needed shade, and the mist generated by the falling water was like nature's air conditioning. This falls is a real hidden gem of the area. I even spotted wolf tracks along the way!

Kakabika Falls

LOCATION: Southeast of Lake Gogebic

ADDRESS/GPS FOR THE FALLS: 46° 20.249′ N, 89° 27.144′ W

DIRECTIONS: Starting in Marenisco at the M-64/US-2 intersection, drive west on US-2 for 12.5 miles. Turn left onto Co. Rd. 527, and drive for 0.5 mile until you come to a small area where you can pull off on the left. Park, and follow the narrow footpath into the woods.

WEBSITE: www.fs.usda.gov/recarea/ottawa/recarea/?recid=12348

WATERWAY: Cisco Branch Ontonagon River

HEIGHT: 14 feet (tallest of 3 cascades)

CREST: Varies

NEAREST TOWN: Marenisco

HIKE DIFFICULTY: Fair, small hills

TRAIL QUALITY: Fair; narrow with tree roots

ROUND-TRIP DISTANCE: 0.4 mile

ADMISSION: No fee

TRIP REPORT & TIPS:

Kakabika Falls is a long, cascading falls with 3 smaller drops along the way. From top to bottom, the elevation drops more than 50 feet. The falls winds through the woods in the shape of an "S," and a narrow footpath leads you along the route. Dark-colored boulders and rocks line the banks; they're covered with bright green moss and ferns, making a nice contrast.

If you visit during the fall colors, the leaves look stunning against the dark rocks and river water. This is a real gem that doesn't get a lot of attention, and it is fairly easy to reach, as it's close to the road.

Cascade Falls

LOCATION: Trap Hills, Ottawa National Forest

ADDRESS/GPS FOR THE FALLS: 46° 39.106′ N, 89° 26.780′ W

DIRECTIONS: From Bergland, drive east on M-28 for 1.3 miles. Turn left onto Forest Road 400. Follow this dirt road for 7.3 miles, and then turn right onto a two-track trail with a sign noting Cascade Falls. Follow for 0.3 mile to parking area.

WEBSITE: www.fs.usda.gov/recarea/ottawa/recreation/hiking/recarea/?recid=12360&actid=50

WATERWAY: Cascade Creek

HEIGHT: 18 feet **CREST:** 18–40 feet

NEAREST TOWN: Bergland

HIKE DIFFICULTY: Fair

TRAIL QUALITY: Fair; muddy, rocky terrain at falls

ROUND-TRIP DISTANCE: 1.4 miles

ADMISSION: No fee

TRIP REPORT & TIPS:

There are two hiking loops here: one leads to the waterfall; the other features the landscape known as the Trap Hills.

When you follow the trail to the falls, at 0.4 mile you will reach a fork where you can continue right to the falls or go left for the Bluff Trail, which will lead you to the overlook of the Trap Hills. Heading toward the falls, you'll hear the falls before actually see it. When you reach it, the trail will lead to a smooth rock outcropping overlooking the large cascade that makes up Cascade Falls. If you make the hike up the Bluff Trail, it's a lot more challenging, but the views are rewarding.

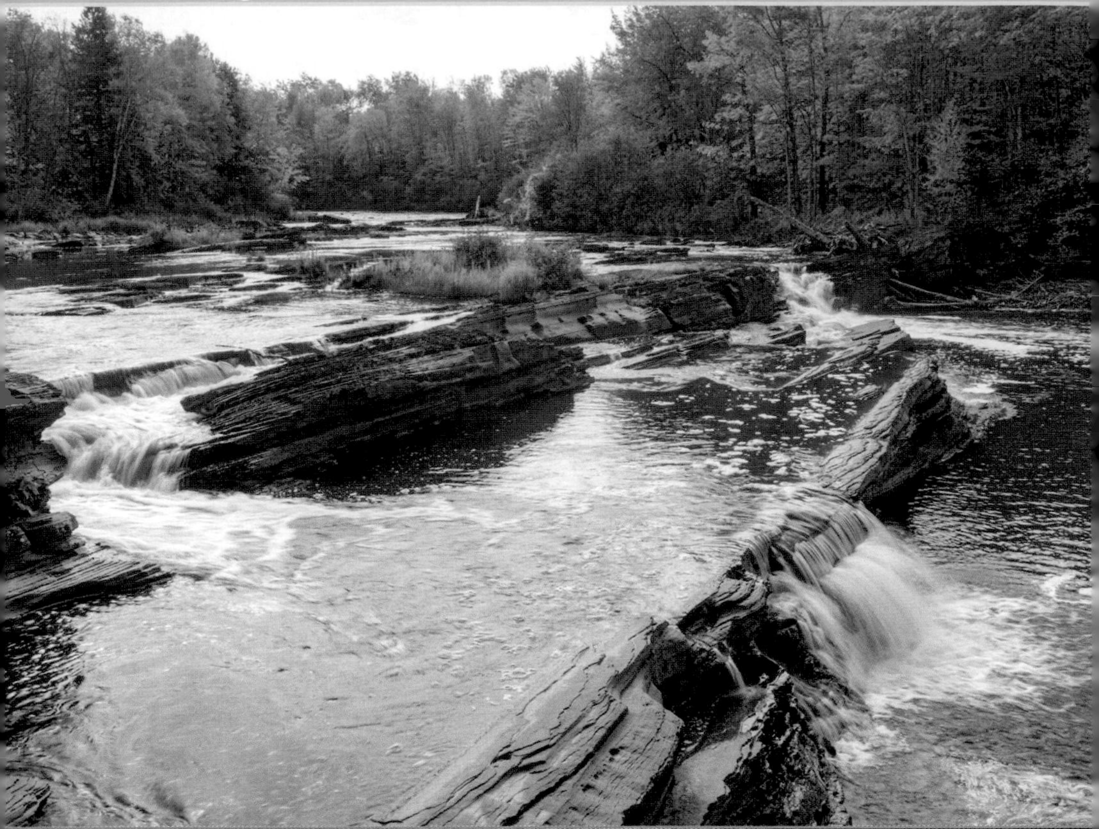

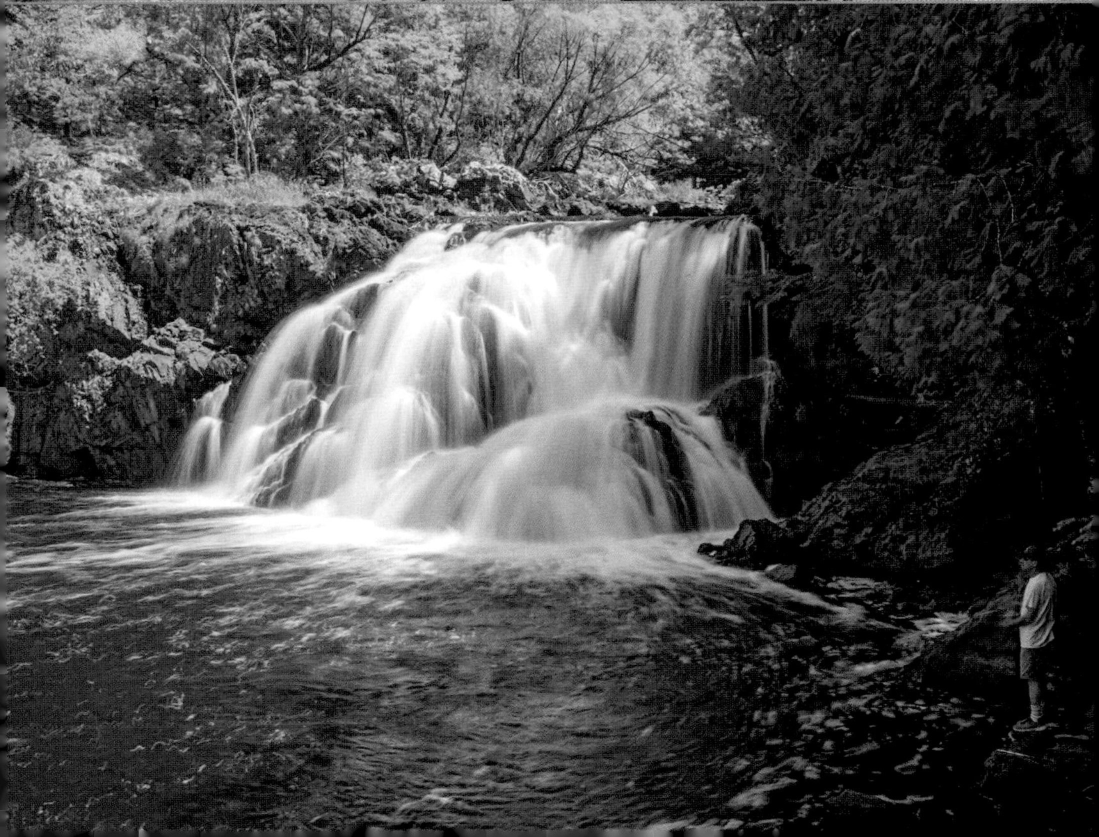

Bonanza Falls

LOCATION: Silver City

ADDRESS/GPS FOR THE FALLS:
46° 49.060′ N, 89° 34.212′ W

DIRECTIONS: From Silver City, drive south on M-64, heading toward White Pine. Follow for 0.9 mile, and turn right at the dirt road. Follow this for 0.1 mile to the large parking area.

WEBSITE: None

WATERWAY: Big Iron River

HEIGHT: 14 feet **CREST:** 30–183 feet, based on water levels

NEAREST TOWN: Silver City

HIKE DIFFICULTY: Easy

TRAIL QUALITY: Good

ROUND-TRIP DISTANCE: 125 yards

ADMISSION: No fee

TRIP REPORT & TIPS:

Bonanza Falls (also referred to as Greenwood Falls) is located just outside of the nearby Porcupine Mountains Wilderness State Park, and is on one of the wider rivers you'll come across in the area. The falls aren't overly dramatic, as they're a multi-level cascade with a narrow chute. I find the slanted layers of shale rock most fascinating. These thin layers create some really neat-looking rock formations, with water flowing in and around them. During the fall, the wide river is lined with some spectacular autumn colors.

If you visit during the spring melt, expect a raging river with water flowing the entire width of the river. It's a completely different—and intense—scene compared to the tranquil summer months.

Interstate Falls

LOCATION: Michigan/Wisconsin border

ADDRESS/GPS FOR THE FALLS: 46° 28.546′ N, 90° 12.055′ W

DIRECTIONS: Starting in Ironwood, follow US-2 across the state border and into Hurley, WI. Continue west on US-2 for another 0.7 mile, and then turn right onto Center Dr. (There is also sign along the road for Peterson Falls.)

WEBSITE: None

WATERWAY: Montreal River

HEIGHT: 18 feet **CREST:** 24 feet

NEAREST TOWN: Ironwood

HIKE DIFFICULTY: Easy (some stairs)

TRAIL QUALITY: Good

ROUND-TRIP DISTANCE: 0.4 mile

ADMISSION: No fee

TRIP REPORT & TIPS:

This falls occurs on the Michigan/Wisconsin state line, but the Michigan side is on private property, so you have to travel to Wisconsin to see it. There's also a little confusion about the name.

After parking, follow the well-maintained trail into the woods. After a short distance, you'll come to a "T" and then head left from here. The path will lead you near the riverbank and over some small hills. Once you get to the falls, there are a few different viewing spots alongside the falls. Head down the medium-size wooden staircase (32 steps) to a really nice viewing platform with bench seating. This is the perfect spot to see the falls and relax in the shadows of the forest.

Powderhorn Falls

LOCATION: Near Powderhorn Ski Resort

ADDRESS/GPS FOR THE FALLS: 46° 30.362′N, 90° 04.925′W

DIRECTIONS: From Bessemer, drive west on US-2, and turn right onto Powderhorn Rd. Follow for 1.8 miles, and park along the right side of the road. If you pass a large lodging building on the right, you have gone too far. The shoulder is a little worn at the falls parking area, and from there a footpath heads into the woods.

WEBSITE: None

WATERWAY: Powder Mill Creek

HEIGHT: 20 feet **CREST:** Varies

NEAREST TOWN: Bessemer

HIKE DIFFICULTY: Easy to difficult

TRAIL QUALITY: Good to fair

ROUND-TRIP DISTANCE: 280 yards

ADMISSION: No fee

TRIP REPORT & TIPS:

Powderhorn Falls is a nice, two-drop falls located a short distance from the road. There are no markings indicating where you'll find the falls. After parking along the road, follow the worn path into the woods. This flat trail leads you directly to a rock overview of the creek and falls. Of the two drops, the upper eight-foot cascade is more easily viewable and accessible. Both drops are next to each other, but because of the creek layout and terrain, the lower one is more difficult to see. The best view of the lower drop is found if you climb down a steep, loose rock hill and then wade across to the opposite bank in order to see the falls. To help get you down that hill, a convenient rope with loop handles has been added by other visitors.

Nelson Canyon Falls

LOCATION: Southwest of Lake Gogebic

ADDRESS/GPS FOR THE FALLS: 46° 23.513′N, 89° 34.780′W

DIRECTIONS: From Marenisco, drive east on US-2 for 5.5 miles to CC Rd. Turn left (north) and drive for 0.9 mile to a two-track trail on the right. The two-track trail also has a National Forest marker noting that the road is closed to vehicle traffic, so be sure to park along the road. If you reach the small bridge, you've gone too far.

WEBSITE: None

WATERWAY: Nelson Creek

HEIGHT: 13 feet **CREST:** 1–8 feet

NEAREST TOWN: Marenisco

HIKE DIFFICULTY: Difficult

TRAIL QUALITY: Poor; the worn path is barely visible

ROUND-TRIP DISTANCE: 2 miles

ADMISSION: No fee

TRIP REPORT & TIPS:

From the main road, walk east on the two-track which seems to end about 0.2 miles into the journey. From here, there isn't much of a trail but walk north till you reach the creek. Now, start following the shallow creek downstream (east). I found staying up on the banks was easier and you may find a worn path. The canyon becomes much more defined as you get closer to the falls with near 50-foot rock cliffs. Once at the top of the falls, scale the steep hill to the river and then work your way back upstream. This waterfall is best viewed in the spring and a GPS is recommended.

Root Beer Falls

LOCATION: Wakefield

ADDRESS/GPS FOR THE FALLS:
46° 29.387′ N, 89° 55.676′ W

DIRECTIONS: Starting in Wakefield, take M-28 for 1.5 miles. You'll pass Sunday Lake and reach Wertanen Rd. Turn left onto this dirt road. Drive for about 300 feet and look to your left. The falls are visible from the road. Park along the shoulder.

WEBSITE: None

WATERWAY: Planter Creek

HEIGHT: 7 feet **CREST:** 25 feet

NEAREST TOWN: Wakefield

HIKE DIFFICULTY: Easy

TRAIL QUALITY: Good

ROUND-TRIP DISTANCE: 250 feet

ADMISSION: No fee

TRIP REPORT & TIPS:

This is a nice, surprising waterfall to visit, as it's just a short distance north of US-2, and it's visible through the trees from the road. Foot traffic to the falls has created a decent trail through the woods that begins along the shoulder. There is a relatively steep bank to descend, but otherwise it's a flat, winding trail to the falls. This creek has another waterfall (Sunday Lake Falls, below), which is one of the more unusual falls I've come across.

Sunday Lake Falls

LOCATION: Wakefield

ADDRESS/GPS FOR THE FALLS:
46° 29.240′ N, 89° 55.900′ W

DIRECTIONS: Starting in Wakefield, take M-28 for 1.3 miles to the Planter Creek bridge. You'll pass Sunday Lake along the way. Park along the highway. To give yourself the most room along the shoulder of the highway, park before or after the guardrail.

WEBSITE: None

WATERWAY: Planter Creek

HEIGHT: 10 feet **CREST:** 40 feet

NEAREST TOWN: Wakefield

HIKE DIFFICULTY: Medium

TRAIL QUALITY: Poor; there's no real trail here

ROUND-TRIP DISTANCE: .15 mile

ADMISSION: No fee

TRIP REPORT & TIPS:

This is one of the most unique waterfalls in this book, as the waterfall begins in a cave—which is actually a manmade tunnel from the mining days! The creek flows underground and then makes its grand entrance at this falls.

Although it's only a short distance from the highway, I didn't have much luck finding a trail, and the terrain is steep in spots. I ended up parking along the highway and walking in the grass toward the creek. I then followed the creek upstream (south side of the highway), staying close to river. It's rocky and jagged but manageable, and it's definitely worth the effort for such a unique falls.

Sturgeon Falls

Sturgeon Falls is located within the Sturgeon River Gorge Wilderness. The gorge is over 300 feet deep and a mile wide.

A narrow chute just upstream of the falls

Sturgeon Falls

Sturgeon Falls is remote, so for those looking to avoid the crowds, this one is for you.

LOCATION: Sturgeon River Gorge Wilderness, Ottawa National Forest

ADDRESS/GPS FOR THE FALLS: 46° 38.561′N, 88° 41.634′W

DIRECTIONS: From M-28 in Sidnaw, drive north on Forest Road 2200 for 12.5 miles, and turn left on Forest Road 2270. Drive for 0.6 mile, and look for parking on the right side of the road. The marked trailhead for the falls begins across the road.

WEBSITE: https://www.fs.usda.gov/recarea/ottawa/recarea/?recid=12322

WATERWAY: Sturgeon River

HEIGHT: 15 feet **CREST:** 22 feet

NEAREST TOWN: Sidnaw

HIKE DIFFICULTY: Difficult with steep hills and rocks

TRAIL QUALITY: Well-maintained trail

ROUND-TRIP DISTANCE: 1.8 miles

ADMISSION: No fee

TRIP REPORT & TIPS:

After visiting this waterfall for the first time, I wondered what took me so long to visit! It has it all: remoteness, a fun adventurous hike, and thundering falls. Your adventure begins with a hike along the edge of the mile-wide, 350-foot-deep gorge that stretches across the landscape. After a quarter mile, the trail starts the descent down into the gorge, with a narrow path and a switchback to help make the steep hill easier to navigate.

The approach to the falls is from above and upstream, so you can see the progression of the 100-foot-wide Sturgeon River being squeezed through a narrow, volcanic outcropping that's only 25 feet wide. During my late-autumn visit, the river was low, but the sound and mist created by the falls was still impressive. (During the spring season, the falls are roaring!) You'll want to use extra caution hiking near the base of the falls, where the rocks and moss are wet and slippery. Beyond the falls, I also hiked downstream a short distance to take in the sight of the towering cliffs and hills across the river.

Because of the challenge and remoteness, I would recommend carrying a supply of snacks and food and only attempting this trek with a decent level of physical fitness. Take your time and enjoy the views!

Angelic light from the sun and mist

Hungarian Falls

Hungarian Falls features three great waterfalls—each with its own unique character.

Middle Falls

Hungarian Falls

Take some time to read the "Geo Tour" signs near the falls. They provide some great details about the geology of the area.

LOCATION: 7 miles northeast of Hancock

ADDRESS/GPS FOR THE FALLS: Upper Falls: 47° 10.442′ N, 88° 27.074′ W; Middle Falls: 47° 10.325′ N, 88° 26.870′ W; Lower Falls: 47° 10.286′ N, 88° 26.832′ W

DIRECTIONS: Starting in Hancock near the lift bridge, drive north on M-26 toward Lake Linden. After 8.1 miles, turn left onto 6th St. in Tamarack City. Drive for 200 feet, and then veer left onto Golf Course Rd. Drive up the steep hill, which turns to dirt, for 0.5 mile. Look for a two-track road on the left blocked by 3 orange metal poles. Park along the road, and walk up the two-track.

WEBSITE: www.keweenawlandtrust.org/special-hungarian-falls.php

WATERWAY: Dover Creek

HEIGHT: Upper Falls: 39 feet (drop and cascade); Middle Falls: 18 feet; Lower Falls: 70 feet **CREST:** Upper Falls: 45 feet, Middle Falls: 12; Lower Falls: 40 feet

NEAREST TOWN: Hubbell

HIKE DIFFICULTY: Fair if you stay on the trail; difficult if you attempt to capture images like those shown here

TRAIL QUALITY: Fair to poor

ROUND-TRIP DISTANCE: 1.2 miles

ADMISSION: No fee

TRIP REPORT & TIPS:

After parking, follow the two-track road into the woods, where it comes to a clearing along Dover Creek. You're now close to the three major falls of Hungarian Falls. I usually start with the Upper Falls and then work my way back down. To reach the Upper Falls, head to the right, which will go past a historic dam and pond as well as signage for the Keweenaw Land Trust. Follow the trail along a ridge, and to the large cascading Upper Falls, which will be visible through the trees. To get the best view (like the one pictured), you'll need to carefully climb down the steep embankment to the river's edge.

To view the Middle Falls, head back down the trail and follow Dover Creek downstream. After a short walk past the dam, you will arrive at the top of the Middle Falls, with a view through the trees of these impressive plunging falls. Again, the best view is down next to the falls, which requires some effort. There is a steep trail near the top of the falls that leads to the large pool below the falls. A less-steep approach (the way I took the photo) is to continue downstream a short ways to where the bank levels out. Here, you can wade across the creek and head back upstream to the large pool and falls.

The Lower Falls are just a short distance from the Middle Falls, but seeing them is difficult. The trail approaches from the top but doesn't give you much of a view. To see the Lower Falls from within the gorge near the base (like pictured), it is very challenging with steep terrain. To do so, follow the river downstream along the top of the gorge, finding a narrow path (there are a few created by past visitors) that leads you down to the river, and then working your way back upstream along the river's edge. Again, this is very challenging, as the terrain is steep and unruly. Use caution if you make an attempt.

Lower Falls

Eagle River Falls

Eagle River Falls is very convenient to see as it's just off the main road and a large foot bridge gives you a great view.

Constructed long ago, the remains of a wooden dam is still intact at the top of the falls

Eagle River Falls

For the lighthouse lovers, I recommend driving to nearby Eagle Harbor to visit the Eagle Harbor Lighthouse.

LOCATION: Eagle River

ADDRESS/GPS FOR THE FALLS: 47° 24.735' N, 88° 17.804'W

DIRECTIONS: Located roadside on M-26 in Eagle River. A small parking area is located just north of the river and falls on a nearby side street.

WEBSITE: None

WATERWAY: Eagle River

HEIGHT: 38 feet **CREST:** Varies; can be 60 feet or more

NEAREST TOWN: Eagle River

HIKE DIFFICULTY: Easy

TRAIL QUALITY: Good, paved

ROUND-TRIP DISTANCE: 250 feet

ADMISSION: No fee

TRIP REPORT & TIPS:

If you're in the Keweenaw area, then Eagle River Falls should be on your must-see list of waterfalls. This is a very nice waterfall with a unique history and features. It also offers the visitor a unique perspective when viewing the falls. The original highway bridge was converted to a pedestrian bridge, so you can easily park and walk to view the falls from above. The newly built arched timber bridge behind you is also worth checking out.

The falls is a large cascade that descends into a gorge below you. Depending on the flow of the river, the river can look vein-like as it winds down the basalt rock. In the middle of the falls are two giant tub-like rock features, which were carved out over time by the swirling water motion.

At the top of the falls you'll also see remnants of an old wooden dam once used by the Lake Superior Safety Fuse Company. The dam diverts most of the water to the right side of the falls. During high water levels, the river will flow the entire width of the open rock face.

Montreal Falls

Located at the northern tip of Michigan, Montreal Falls features three unique waterfalls in a very remote U.P. wilderness setting.

Middle Falls

Montreal Falls

The 1.4-mile hike to the Lower Falls follows the Lake Superior shoreline and offers some great scenery along the way.

LOCATION: 8 miles east of Lac La Belle

ADDRESS/GPS FOR THE FALLS: Lower: 47° 23.549′ N, 87° 50.496′ W; Middle: 47° 23.720′ N, 87° 50.129′ W; Upper: 47° 23.877′ N, 87° 50.185′ W

DIRECTIONS: Starting in Copper Harbor, take US-41 south for 10.6 miles, and turn left on Lac La Belle Rd. After driving past Mount Bohemia ski hill, you'll come to a "Y"; take the left fork (Bete Grise Rd.). Continue for 3 miles, and turn left onto Smith Fisheries Rd., following this wide dirt road. Along the way, you'll see a sign indicating that this is a private road. The owners have kindly opened it to the public. Please be respectful. Continuing, stay on this main road, past the two-tracks and driveways along the way, for 5.3 miles. This dirt road has some very steep parts and is bumpy; park near the stone-and-wood fence line.

WEBSITE: None

WATERWAY: Montreal River

HEIGHT: Lower: 19 feet; Middle: 15 feet; Upper: 10 feet **CREST:** Lower: 45 feet; Middle: 12 feet; Upper: 10 feet

NEAREST TOWN: Lac La Belle

HIKE DIFFICULTY: Lower: Easy; Middle: Fair; Upper: Difficult

TRAIL QUALITY: Lower: Fair, mud; Middle: Fair, hills/tree roots; Upper: Poor, faint trail

ROUND-TRIP DISTANCE: Lower: 2.8 miles; Middle: 3.8 miles (0.5 mile beyond Lower); Upper: 4.6 miles (0.4 mile beyond Middle)

ADMISSION: None

TRIP REPORT & TIPS:

Lower Falls: From the parking area, head down the wide two-track, and a walking path is off to the left and follows the lakeshore. Along the way, the trail becomes narrower, and you'll need to navigate over downed trees and through muddy spots. Within a short distance of the lower falls, the trail will come out of the woods and into an open area with a great panoramic view of the shoreline. The view to the west is stunning, with the Bare Bluff rock cliff being the centerpiece! The Lower Falls is right at the mouth, with large and wild multi-drop cascades flowing directly into Lake Superior.

Middle Falls: After taking in the Lower Falls, follow the path upstream. The trail stays close to the river and passes some scenic pools and rapids and gets hillier. You'll hear Middle Falls, before you see it. The approach is on a high bank across from the falls. To get a clear view, you'll need to scurry down the bank.

Upper Falls: Continuing past the Middle Falls, the trail leads up a steep, rocky hill, and you'll find yourself up on the cliff above Middle Falls. From here, the trail becomes less defined and narrower. For the most part, the trail stays close to the river, but there are slippery hills and downed trees. I found myself losing track of the trail and re-finding it. Once you reach the falls, the view is more from the side. To get to the top of the falls, follow the conglomerate rock cliff at the base.

Lower Falls

Hogger Falls

West Branch Sturgeon Falls

Hogger Falls & West Branch Sturgeon Falls

LOCATION: Ottawa National Forest

ADDRESS/GPS FOR THE FALLS: Hogger Falls: 46° 43.422′ N, 88° 48.255′ W; West Branch Sturgeon Falls: 46° 43.300′ N, 88° 47.928′ W

DIRECTIONS: From Nisula, drive west on M-38 for 0.9 mile, and turn left (south) on Newberry Rd. Follow for 2.9 miles, and park at the second gated two-track road on the left. If you reach the river, you've gone too far. **Note:** The last 2 miles are on a seasonal road.

WEBSITE: www.fs.usda.gov/ottawa

WATERWAY: West Branch Sturgeon River

HEIGHT: Hogger Falls: 10 feet; West Branch Sturgeon Falls: 7 feet **CREST:** Hogger Falls: 20 feet; West Branch Sturgeon Falls: 30 feet

NEAREST TOWN: Nisula

HIKE DIFFICULTY: Hogger Falls: Fair; West Branch Sturgeon Falls: Fair to difficult

TRAIL QUALITY: Hogger Falls: Good, but no trail; West Branch Sturgeon Falls: Good, but no trail

ROUND-TRIP DISTANCE: Hogger Falls: 1.2 miles; West Branch Sturgeon Falls: 2 miles

ADMISSION: No fee

TRIP REPORT & TIPS:

To reach the first (and biggest and farthest) West Branch Sturgeon Falls, follow the two-track east past the gate for 0.9 mile. Look for another faded two-track road to the right and follow. This will lead you directly to the waterfall. To see the other four smaller falls, just follow the river back upstream. Because of the distance between the last waterfall and Hogger Falls, you may find it easier to reconnect with the two-track road and follow it the short way back toward your vehicle. Then use a GPS and the waypoint to find Hogger Falls.

Here's how to find Hogger Falls when starting from your vehicle: Walk beyond the gate and head east down the two-track road for 0.5 mile. At this point turn south (right) into the woods. Blaze your own trail through the woods for 175 yards, where you'll come to the river. You should be able to hear (or see) Hogger Falls from there. During my spring visit, the water was flowing high, and a late-April snowstorm added to the scenery.

Fenner's Falls

LOCATION: Phoenix

ADDRESS/GPS FOR THE FALLS: 47° 24.242′N, 88° 17.612′W

DIRECTIONS: From US-41 in Phoenix, follow M-26 (driving toward Eagle River) for 1.4 miles. There will be a driveway on the left and a white mailbox on the right. Park along the shoulder, just before the mailbox. Look for a narrow footpath on the right leading into the woods.

WEBSITE: None

WATERWAY: Eagle River

HEIGHT: 25 feet **CREST:** 15–45 feet

NEAREST TOWN: Phoenix

HIKE DIFFICULTY: Very difficult

TRAIL QUALITY: Fair to poor

ROUND-TRIP DISTANCE: 400 feet

ADMISSION: No fee

TRIP REPORT & TIPS:

Although the distance to the falls is short, actually getting there is another story. Once you find the narrow footpath at the road, follow it into the woods until you come to a steep descent. This is where it becomes a real challenge and potentially dangerous, but the path is well worn. **Use caution.** The path narrows and is nearly vertical in spots. If you want to get there, you'll need to cling to tree roots and limbs in order to climb down. It took me a few tries to find my footing, as well as work up the bravery.

Once you do reach the falls, it is a rather impressive setting, with two main drops in a rocky canyon. The upper drop goes through a narrow chute and is around 10 feet long, before it levels out to a small pool. From here the river widens and then makes another descent down a 12-foot cascade. Overall, it is a very pretty and wild setting.

Jacobs Falls

LOCATION: 3 miles northeast of Eagle River

ADDRESS/GPS FOR THE FALLS: 47° 25.680′ N, 88° 14.264′ W

DIRECTIONS: Starting in Eagle River, drive northeast on M-26 for 3 miles. Jacobs Falls will be along the road on the right. A wide shoulder is available for parking across the road on the left.

WEBSITE: None

WATERWAY: Jacobs Creek

HEIGHT: 28 feet **CREST:** 5–10 feet

NEAREST TOWN: Eagle River

HIKE DIFFICULTY: Roadside

TRAIL QUALITY: Roadside

ROUND-TRIP DISTANCE: 50 feet

ADMISSION: No fee

TRIP REPORT & TIPS:

Jacobs Falls is one of my favorite roadside waterfalls and one of the closest to the road. The waterfall is a long slide into a shallow pool and then disappears under the road. Looking above the falls, you can see another drop and there are also a couple more falls upstream if you're feeling adventurous. A steep, worn path along the left side will lead you to them.

During a visit in early August, the thimbleberries were red ripe and plentiful along the base of the falls. Speaking of berries, the famous Jampot is just a couple hundred feet up the road from the falls. This unique little shop sells jams, jellies and baked goods made (and operated) by monks of the Holy Transfiguration Skete.

Wyandotte Falls

LOCATION: Twin Lakes

ADDRESS/GPS FOR THE FALLS:
46° 53.435' N, 88° 52.758' W

DIRECTIONS: From the Twin Lakes area on M-26, head west on Poyhonen Rd. past Omer's Golf Course. Drive for 0.8 mile, and look for a small parking area on the left, just past the golf course maintenance buildings.

WEBSITE: None

WATERWAY: Misery River

HEIGHT: 15 feet **CREST:** 7–12 feet

NEAREST TOWN: Twin Lakes

HIKE DIFFICULTY: Fair

TRAIL QUALITY: Good, but there are tree roots, rocks, and slopes

ROUND-TRIP DISTANCE: 245 yards

ADMISSION: No fee

TRIP REPORT & TIPS:

If you're near the Twin Lakes area south of Houghton, Wyandotte Falls is a lesser-known cascading falls worth checking out. After parking, just follow the footpath into the woods, which winds its way through a young forest and to the top of falls. The trail then continues down the side of the falls to the base.

During my visit in the early spring, snow could still be found in the woods, and the river was really flowing. I've heard that during the hot summer months this falls can slow down to a small trickle. I would recommend making a visit during the spring and early summer months to see this cascade on the Misery River.

Ten Foot Falls

LOCATION: Phoenix

ADDRESS/GPS FOR THE FALLS:
47° 23.852' N, 88° 17.073 W

DIRECTIONS: From US-41 in Phoenix, follow M-26 (driving north toward Eagle River) for 0.8 mile. The waterfall and the parking area are on the right side of the road.

WEBSITE: None

WATERWAY: Eagle River

HEIGHT: 8 feet **CREST:** 30 feet

NEAREST TOWN: Phoenix

HIKE DIFFICULTY: Easy

TRAIL QUALITY: Good

ROUND-TRIP DISTANCE: 100 yards

ADMISSION: No fee

TRIP REPORT & TIPS:

Hidden just a bit from the road, this waterfall is just a short distance from the parking area. Just follow the well-worn path a short distance to the river, and you are at the top of the falls! The falls cascades through a large mix of dark rock, before flowing into a very large, clear pool. During the summer, this is a very popular place to relax in the cool river water and wade in the clear pool below the falls.

Silver River Falls

LOCATION: Between Eagle Harbor and Copper Harbor

ADDRESS/GPS FOR THE FALLS: 47° 27.798′ N, 88° 04.375′ W

DIRECTIONS: Starting in Eagle Harbor, follow M-26 east for 4.5 miles, heading toward Copper Harbor. Park in the dirt circle loop just before the Silver River bridge on the right. Cross the road to reach the falls.

WEBSITE: None

WATERWAY: Silver River

HEIGHT: Upper portion: 15 feet; lower portion: 8 feet **CREST:** 20–30 feet

NEAREST TOWN: Eagle Harbor

HIKE DIFFICULTY: Fair

TRAIL QUALITY: Fair

ROUND-TRIP DISTANCE: 0.2 mile

ADMISSION: No fee

TRIP REPORT & TIPS:

Silver River Falls is a unique waterfall, thanks to its two different styles of drops and the unique stone bridge found nearby. The upper portion is a long sloping falls over levels of conglomerate rock. The river then levels out for a short distance, before there are a couple more drops over a different type of rock.

To view it, just cross the road and follow the stone stairs into the woods. A narrow footpath then leads you along the river as it descends down a sloping rock face. Looking back upstream, you will see the unique bridge, with its stonework and arch. The path then continues to the bottom, where the river and landscape level out.

Manganese Falls

LOCATION: Less than a mile south of Copper Harbor

ADDRESS/GPS FOR THE FALLS: 47° 27.699′ N, 87° 52.734′ W

DIRECTIONS: Starting in Copper Harbor on US-41, head south on Manganese Rd. Drive for 0.7 mile, past Lake Fanny Hooe, and look for a wider shoulder area on the right to park. There is also a sign that marks the location of the falls.

WEBSITE: None

WATERWAY: Manganese Creek

HEIGHT: 35 feet **CREST:** 15 feet

NEAREST TOWN: Copper Harbor

HIKE DIFFICULTY: Easy

TRAIL QUALITY: Good, with some tree roots

ROUND-TRIP DISTANCE: 240 feet

ADMISSION: No fee

TRIP REPORT & TIPS:

During my visit, I tried a few different vantage points to get a look at this falls from top to bottom. The view when you're down in the gorge is interesting enough, but it's not worth the effort if you're trying to see the waterfall. There is one platform area for viewing the falls through the trees, but the best view is a little bit farther upstream, where the river makes its descent. The water here flows through rounded conglomerate rock to form some pretty neat ribbons.

Reaching the top of the falls is easy. After parking, head across the road and past the wooden sign. Then, follow the footpath to the right. This follows the rim of the gorge, where the stream begins its descent.

Haven Falls

LOCATION: Lac La Belle

ADDRESS/GPS FOR THE FALLS:
47° 22.912' N, 88° 01.720' W

DIRECTIONS: Starting in Copper Harbor, take US-41 south for 10.6 miles, and turn left on Lac La Belle Rd. After driving past Mount Bohemia ski hill, you'll come to a "Y" and stay to the right. Drive another 0.5 mile, and look for the Haven Falls Park and the falls on the right.

WEBSITE: None

WATERWAY: Haven Creek

HEIGHT: 22 feet **CREST:** 16 feet

NEAREST TOWN: Lac La Belle

HIKE DIFFICULTY: Roadside

TRAIL QUALITY: Good

ROUND-TRIP DISTANCE: 180 feet

ADMISSION: No fee

TRIP REPORT & TIPS:

Haven Falls is located just south of the quaint little town of Lac La Belle, on the eastern side of the Keweenaw Peninsula. The falls is visible from the road, but there's also a nice little park with benches, picnic tables, grills, pit toilets, and a nice pavilion nearby. The falls have a very steep slide and an upper portion that's hidden from view. After the falls, the creek flows through the park and into the nearby lake, Lac La Belle.

It's also worth noting that a visit to Bete Grise beach on Lake Superior is a short distance away and worth the stop. The sandy beach and the nearby rugged landscape to the north are quite the sight!

Madison Gap Falls

LOCATION: 1 mile south of Eagle Harbor

ADDRESS/GPS FOR THE FALLS: 47° 26.379' N, 88° 09.946' W

DIRECTIONS: In Eagle Harbor, take Eagle Harbor Cut Off Rd. south of town for 1.1 miles. Just before Eliza Creek, turn left and park in a small clearing. The waterfall is across the road.

WEBSITE: None

WATERWAY: Eliza Creek

HEIGHT: 18 feet **CREST:** 3 feet

NEAREST TOWN: Eagle Harbor

HIKE DIFFICULTY: Moderate

TRAIL QUALITY: Nonexistent; you'll be bushwhacking

ROUND-TRIP DISTANCE: 200 yards

ADMISSION: No fee

TRIP REPORT & TIPS:

This waterfall is best viewed during the wet seasons, as I've seen it dry up in midsummer. The falls begin with the creek being squeezed into a narrow rocky chute. It then makes its way to a wider, calmer pool at the base.

Getting to the falls doesn't take long, but it does require some trailblazing, as there is no trail. After crossing the paved road, make your way through a treeline to a clearing for a power line. Head to the right, and at the second pole, turn left into the woods. Walk down the steep bank, and the base of the falls will be to your left, a short distance away. Using a GPS to find this waterfall is recommended.

Gratiot River Falls

LOCATION: Ahmeek

ADDRESS/GPS FOR THE FALLS:
47° 20.119′ N, 88° 26.654′ W

DIRECTIONS: In Ahmeek, follow Hubbell St. west for 2 blocks, and then turn right on Bollman St. Follow this north for 0.8 mile (it becomes 5 Mile Point Rd. along the way), then turn left onto a dirt road, which is just before the cemetery on the right. Drive for 0.9 mile, and you'll come to a dirt intersection with Bumbletown Rd. Turn right and follow for 1.9 miles. Portions of this road can be narrow and rough in spots. Look for a two-track trail leading into the woods on the right, and park along Bumbletown Rd.

WEBSITE: None

WATERWAY: Gratiot River

HEIGHT: Main falls: 7 feet; upper cascade: 5 feet
CREST: 40 feet

NEAREST TOWN: Ahmeek

HIKE DIFFICULTY: Fair

TRAIL QUALITY: Fair to poor

ROUND-TRIP DISTANCE: 0.4 mile

ADMISSION: No fee

TRIP REPORT & TIPS:

Also known as Lower Gratiot River Falls, this is a nice side trip if you're enroute to the County Park, a wonderful Lake Superior destination about a mile further on Bumbletown Rd. After parking along the road, walk the two-track into the woods. After a ways, you'll come to a fork, and you'll want to stay to the right, which leads down a larger hill and then a smaller hill just before you reach the falls. The main drop is straight ahead and a gradual cascade is just upstream.

Queen Anne's Falls

LOCATION: Northeast of Calumet

ADDRESS/GPS FOR THE FALLS:
47° 16.492′ N, 88° 23.370′ W

DIRECTIONS: From Calumet, drive north on US-41 to Allouez, and turn right on Allouez-Copper City Rd. (1st St.). Drive for 0.5 mile and park along the shoulder near the snowmobile/ATV trail (trail #3) on the right. Follow this trail south. **Note**: This trail is dedicated to ATVs only; no cars or trucks allowed.

WEBSITE: None

WATERWAY: Slaughterhouse Creek

HEIGHT: 27 feet **CREST:** 3–5 feet

NEAREST TOWN: Copper City

HIKE DIFFICULTY: Easy to difficult

TRAIL QUALITY: Good to poor

ROUND-TRIP DISTANCE: 1.6 miles

ADMISSION: No fee

TRIP REPORT & TIPS:

To visit this relatively unknown but impressive waterfall, walk south on the mentioned ORV trail for 0.3 mile. Continue left here while the ORV trail veers to the right. After 0.2 mile, look for a narrower, sandy two-track to the left which leads up a small hill. Follow this trail, and always stay to the right when you come to a "Y." After the trail heads into the woods, it will come to a clearing. On the opposite side, follow the narrow footpath which leads down a very steep, rutted and worn hill. Take your time to reach the base.

Penn Falls (Upper & Lower)

LOCATION: East of Ontonagon

ADDRESS/GPS FOR THE FALLS:
Lower Penn Falls: 46° 49.561′ N, 88° 57.655′ W;
Upper Penn Falls: 46° 49.576′ N, 88° 57.617′ W

DIRECTIONS: From the M-26/M-38 intersection in Lake Mine, head north on M-26 for 3.8 miles. Turn right on the unmarked dirt road, and follow for 0.4 mile, to where it runs into the Bill Nicholls multi-use state trail. (You do not need a special sticker/permit to drive a licensed vehicle on this trail.) Turn left (north) and drive for 1.5 miles to an ATV trail leading into the woods on the right. Park and hike in from here. If you're driving a 4x4, high-clearance vehicle, you can get closer, but the trails can be muddy. For the 4x4s, drive 0.3 mile farther, and turn right on the next dirt road. Follow this two-track trail for 0.6 mile, taking rights at all the forks you encounter, and then parking in a grassy clearing.

WEBSITE: None

WATERWAY: East Branch Firesteel River

HEIGHT: Lower Penn Falls: 7 feet; Upper Penn Falls: 9 feet **CREST:** Lower Penn Falls: 27 feet; Upper Penn Falls: 42 feet

NEAREST TOWN: Lake Mine

HIKE DIFFICULTY: Fair to poor; muddy with stream crossing

TRAIL QUALITY: Fair to poor; ATV trail to no trail

ROUND-TRIP DISTANCE: 1.3 miles if parking along multi-use trail; 0.5 mile if driving and following the second part of the directions

ADMISSION: No fee

TRIP REPORT & TIPS:

After parking along the MI DNR's Bill Nicholls multi-use trail, follow the ATV trail east into the woods. The trail has some small hills, but the main obstacle is getting around the slick mudholes that are often present. This mud is very slick, so use caution to navigate around them. Before getting to the falls, you'll come to a small clearing and a "Y" intersection. Just follow the right fork, which is well worn. (**Note:** This spot is the parking area mentioned in the 4x4 directions at left.) Continuing on, this two-track will lead you down to the river and end at the lower falls.

After enjoying the view of the lower falls, you'll need to wade the stream to see the upper falls, because the bank becomes very steep on this side of the river. Crossing usually isn't difficult, either, as the river is shallow, hard-bottomed, and pretty level. Once you cross, there isn't much of a trail, but the forest is relatively easy to navigate, as you only need to go about 100 yards to reach the upper falls.

Presque Isle River Waterfalls

Like Lake of the Clouds, these waterfalls are another must-see attraction while visiting the Porcupine Mountains.

Nawadaha Falls

Manido Falls

Presque Isle River Waterfalls

Don't miss the details in the bedrock. Over time, the water and loose stones have carved some impressive features in the river bed.

LOCATION: Presque Isle River Scenic Site, Porcupine Mountains Wilderness State Park

ADDRESS/GPS FOR THE FALLS: Nawadaha Falls: 46° 41.971′N, 89° 58.406′W; Manido Falls: 46° 42.246′N, 89° 58.255′W; Manabezho Falls: 46° 42.309′N, 89° 58.254′W; the Potholes: 46° 42.509′N, 89° 58.384′W

DIRECTIONS: From Wakefield, at the M-28/US-2 light, follow M-28 east past Sunday Lake. After 1.3 miles, turn left onto Thomaston Rd. (Co. Rd. 519) and head north. Drive for 15.6 miles, and continue straight (north) past the South Boundary Rd. intersection. Continuing on, you'll see signs for the scenic area and a ranger station. Parking for the uppermost waterfall is near the entrance station. A middle parking area is 0.3 mile past the ranger station, and the final one is 0.5 mile later, at the end of the drive.

WEBSITE: www.dnr.state.mi.us/parksandtrails/Details.aspx?id=426&type=SPRK

WATERWAY: Presque Isle River

HEIGHT: Nawadaha Falls: 15 feet; Manido Falls: 18 feet; Manabezho Falls: 23 feet; the Potholes: 12 feet **CREST:** Nawadaha Falls: 115 feet; Manido Falls: 144 feet; Manabezho Falls: 160 feet; the Potholes: 20 feet

NEAREST TOWN: Wakefield

HIKE DIFFICULTY: Nawadaha Falls: Easy, handicapped accessible; Manido Falls, Manabezho Falls, the Potholes: Fair, but with stairs present

TRAIL QUALITY: Good; maintained path and boardwalks

ROUND-TRIP DISTANCE: Nawadaha Falls: 0.2 mile (parking at ranger station); Manido Falls, Manabezho Falls and the Potholes: 1.2 miles

ADMISSION: Michigan Recreation Passport required (see page 12)

TRIP REPORT & TIPS:

These four impressive waterfalls are located on the Presque Isle River on the far western edge of the Porcupine Mountains. Here, the wide, wild river flows over ledges, drops, and slides, before reaching Lake Superior, nearly a mile later. The state park has done a nice job making these falls accessible, with expansive boardwalks, paths, and a very cool suspension bridge. The uppermost waterfall (Nawadaha Falls) is the only wheelchair-accessible falls; the others require several stairs to reach the boardwalk along the river.

Nawadaha Falls: This waterfall is the farthest upstream of the set. It is located a short distance behind the ranger station, near where you first enter the scenic area. There is a convenient, well-signed parking area across from the ranger station, and a groomed path will lead you to the river and then upstream to the cascading falls. From the observation deck, you'll see the falls through the trees. The best view is along the river, but with the steep terrain, it can be very challenging to get to the river.

Manido Falls, Manabezho Falls, and the Potholes: These three waterfalls are the main attractions of the Scenic Site, and each is unique. As noted in the directions, there are a couple different parking options, depending if you start upstream and head toward Lake Superior, or downstream and work your way back up. I prefer the first option, starting upstream at Manido Falls and working my way down toward the Potholes and Lake Superior.

After parking at the middle parking area, 0.3 mile past the ranger station, head into the woods toward the river, and a set of stairs will take you down to the

Manabezho Falls

The Potholes

TRIP REPORT (CONTINUED): river toward the right. Continue past the crest of Manabezho Falls, and follow the boardwalk to the Manido Falls observation deck. The view here provides an overhead perspective of this large, square-shaped pattern of cascades. For an up-close view, head out onto the riverbed if the river conditions permit. There are some really neat carved shapes in the bedrock, as well as the many layers of Nonesuch Shale at the base of the falls.

Head back on the boardwalk, and next you'll arrive at Manabezho Falls. They are the largest in the scenic area and feature a picturesque sheer drop. The viewing area from the crest feels very much like Upper Tahquamenon Falls, as you can get right up to the edge. For a better overall view, you can follow the boardwalk downstream to where a clearing through the trees provides a distant overall view looking upstream. Although there is no trail to the base of the falls, it is possible to scale the hillside and reach the river. The terrain, though, is steep, muddy, and very difficult to navigate.

Continuing downstream along the boardwalk will lead you to the river's final cascade before it flows into Lake Superior. (A set of stairs will intersect with a very large staircase and you'll want to head to the right, down toward the river and bridge.) Here, an island narrows the river, forcing it through a small gorge, where you'll find some of the most interesting bedrock around. Over time, the rushing water and loose stone have created large bowls (or "potholes"), causing the river to swirl in circular motions. It's a beautiful sight, and one of the most well-known areas of the Porcupine Mountains. The best time to visit is during lower water levels, as more detail will be visible. This is also where the cool wooden suspension bridge is located, which conveniently gives you a great upstream perspective of the Potholes. Although this is the last waterfall, you can continue across the bridge and head a short distance to the Lake Superior shore.

If you're looking for a nice picnic area or restrooms, take the very large staircase, again, all the way to the top. This will lead you to the final parking lot. This area features picnic tables, grills, a covered pavilion and pit toilets.

Black River Scenic Byway Waterfalls

After seeing the five waterfalls along the route, make sure to visit Black River Harbor at the end of the Scenic Byway.

Great Conglomerate Falls

Potawatomi Falls

Black River Scenic Byway Waterfalls

Enroute to the Scenic Byway you'll pass the Copper Peak ski flying jump—the largest in the western Hemisphere. Dare to take a ride to the top?

LOCATION: Black River National Forest Scenic Byway, Ottawa National Forest

ADDRESS/GPS FOR THE FALLS: Great Conglomerate Falls: 46° 37.917′ N, 90° 03.303′ W; Potawatomi Falls: 46° 38.298′ N, 90° 03.080′ W; Gorge Falls: 46° 38.425′ N, 90° 03.014′ W; Sandstone Falls: 46° 39.006′ N, 90° 02.857′ W; Rainbow Falls: 46° 39.538′ N, 90° 02.624′ W

DIRECTIONS: From Bessemer, drive west on US-2 for 1.5 miles, and turn right onto Powderhorn Rd. Follow Powderhorn Rd. for 3 miles (turning right at the ski resort) to where it runs into Black River Rd. (Co. Rd. 513). Turn left and follow for 9.7 miles. There will be a sign for the waterfall parking area on the right for the first waterfall, Great Conglomerate Falls. The four remaining waterfalls are located along the Scenic Byway and are well marked by signs.

WEBSITE: www.fs.usda.gov/ottawa

WATERWAY: Black River

HEIGHT: Great Conglomerate Falls: 20 feet; Potawatomi Falls: 30 feet; Gorge Falls: 27 feet; Sandstone Falls: 14 feet; Rainbow Falls: 46 feet **CREST:** Great Conglomerate Falls: 55 feet and 42 feet (split falls); Potawatomi Falls: 30 feet and 60 feet (split falls); Gorge Falls: 15 feet; Sandstone Falls: 30 feet; Rainbow Falls: 40 feet

NEAREST TOWN: Bessemer

HIKE DIFFICULTY: Great Conglomerate Falls: Medium; Potawatomi Falls: Fair to easy (from Gorge Falls parking it is barrier-free); Gorge Falls: Fair; Sandstone Falls: Medium; Rainbow Falls: Fair to moderate

TRAIL QUALITY: Great Conglomerate Falls: Fair; Potawatomi Falls: Good; Gorge Falls: Good; Sandstone Falls: Fair; Rainbow Falls: Fair

ROUND-TRIP DISTANCE: Great Conglomerate Falls: 1 mile; Potawatomi Falls: 0.2 mile from own parking area, or short barrier-free walk from Gorge Falls parking; Gorge Falls: 250 yards; Sandstone Falls: 0.4 mile; Rainbow Falls: 0.4 mile from Black River Rd. or 1.6 miles from Black River Harbor

ADMISSION: No fee

TRIP REPORT & TIPS:

Black River Falls consists of five unique waterfalls on the Black River, which is part of the 11-mile Black River National Forest Scenic Byway. These five water-falls are some of the best Michigan has to offer. Throw in picturesque Black River Harbor, at the mouth of the Black River on Lake Superior, and you have a real gem of a destination. Whether you decide to see all five or just a few of them, you will be in awe. Below is a breakdown of each waterfall as you drive the Scenic Byway.

Great Conglomerate Falls: From the parking area, follow the nice descend-ing trail through the forest as it leads to the Black River. Once you reach the falls, you are greeted with a great view overlooking the waterfall. Here, the wide Black River is divided by a large conglomerate rock island, with cascading waterfalls on each side.

Potawatomi Falls and Gorge Falls: If you're short on time or have limited mobility, then a visit to these waterfalls is your best choice. Each waterfall has its own parking area, but I recommend just parking at the Gorge Falls parking area, as you can easily see both falls from this lot. This option also provides barrier-free access to view Potawatomi Falls—the only such falls along the

Gorge Falls

Sandstone Falls

Rainbow Falls (view from the alternate route)

TRIP REPORT (CONTINUED): Scenic Byway. From the Gorge Falls parking area, just head to the right to see Potawatomi Falls. It features a great upstream view of the Black River and the cascading waterfall over conglomerate rock. I really love the way the water flows over the bedrock here like thin ribbons.

For **Gorge Falls**, there is series of boardwalks, stairs, and a few different viewing platforms. One option provides a straight-on view of this narrow waterfall and the upstream gorge. The way the water drops effortlessly is unique compared to the other falls. I also like to visit the other viewing area just a short ways upstream from here. From there, you see the gorge near Gorge Falls, as well as gain a great upstream vantage point for viewing Potawatomi Falls.

Sandstone Falls: This waterfall is the smallest of the bunch but worth spotting for its odd shape. Here, the water flows through a wide channel before cascading over large chunks of bedrock. The trail leading there isn't long but does have several trail steps. The trail here also takes you directly to the river's edge, unlike the others. It's fun to walk around on the rock next to the falls and see it up close.

Rainbow Falls: If I had to pick a favorite of the Black River waterfalls, this one would be it. But, there's a catch. For the best view, you have to take the longer, alternate hike in order to see and admire it from the eastern bank of the Black River. You do have the option to see it from the western side, like the other waterfalls here, but the view is very limited and really not worth the effort to me. To reach the eastern bank, follow the Scenic Byway road to the end and park at Black River Harbor. From there, cross the cool wooden suspension bridge that spans the Black River, and then follow the hiking trail back upstream to Rainbow Falls. This hike is long compared to the other falls but not overly difficult. There are a few hills, but it's well maintained and marked. At this vantage point, you get a great, unobstructed view of the falls as it makes its final plunge, before eventually flowing into Lake Superior.

Union River Falls

Lower Union River Falls

Little Union Gorge Falls

Union River Falls & Little Union Gorge Falls

LOCATION: Porcupine Mountains Wilderness State Park

ADDRESS/GPS FOR THE FALLS: Union River Falls: 46° 47.696′ N, 89° 37.673′ W; Lower Union River Falls: 46° 47.850′ N, 89° 37.435′ W; Little Union Gorge Falls: 46° 47.630′ N, 89° 37.399′ W

DIRECTIONS: Leaving the Porcupine Mountains Visitor Center, turn right on S. Boundary Rd. Drive south for 1.4 miles, and turn right into the Union Mine Interpretive Trail parking area. After parking, walk past the sign and the giant shovel to the walking trail beyond it.

WEBSITE: www.michigandnr.com/parksandtrails/Details.aspx?type=SPRK&id=426

WATERWAY: Union River and Little Union River

HEIGHT: Union River Falls: 6 feet; Lower Union River Falls: 70-foot cascade with a 10-foot slide at the bottom; Little Union Gorge Falls: 17 feet **CREST:** Union River Falls: 14 feet; Lower Union River Falls: 24 feet; Little Union Gorge Falls: 20–25 feet

NEAREST TOWN: Silver City

HIKE DIFFICULTY: Fair

TRAIL QUALITY: Good

ROUND-TRIP DISTANCE: 1.1-mile interpretive loop

ADMISSION: Michigan Recreation Passport required (see page 12)

TRIP REPORT & TIPS:

Union River Falls: This is the first falls you'll see on the trail. Its unique history is what makes it intriguing; its right half was the site of a waterwheel long ago.

Lower Union River Falls: Continuing downstream, and across the road, the river begins dropping (nearly 100-feet elevation) more rapidly, and the numerous falls begin. The long final descent is what I'm calling lower falls. To see this one, just head down to the river from where the trail turns into the woods.

Little Union Gorge Falls: Continuing on the interpretive trail, it will lead you to the top of a narrow gorge and the Little Union River—a smaller river but more rugged than the first. Straight ahead is the falls but there is also another similar gorge falls as you continue to the right on the main trail.

Both rivers are best viewed in the spring season.

Trap Falls

LOCATION: Porcupine Mountains Wilderness State Park

ADDRESS/GPS FOR THE FALLS: 46° 47.529′ N, 89° 41.431′ W

DIRECTIONS: Leaving the Porcupine Mountains Visitor Center, turn left onto South Boundary Rd. Drive for 0.3 mile to 107th Engineers Memorial Hwy (M-107). Turn left (west) and drive for 3.5 miles to the Government Peak trailhead parking lot.

WEBSITE: www.michigandnr.com/parksandtrails/Details.aspx?type=SPRK&id=426

WATERWAY: Carp River Inlet

HEIGHT: 16 feet **CREST:** 15–30 feet

NEAREST TOWN: Silver City

HIKE DIFFICULTY: Moderate, hills

TRAIL QUALITY: Fair to poor, muddy, with rocks and tree roots

ROUND-TRIP DISTANCE: 4.2 miles

ADMISSION: Michigan Recreation Passport required (see page 12)

TRIP REPORT & TIPS:

I really enjoyed the hike to Trap Falls, as it has a little bit of everything. The only thing missing is a grand view of the Porcupine Mountains, but there are plenty of other trails and even side trails along the way that provide a fine view of the mountains. There are also other routes to reach Trap Falls, but I chose the Government Peak Trail because it is the shortest route to the falls.

The hike begins up a rocky slope, but luckily this terrain ends after a short ways and becomes smoother. The trail then passes through towering trees with small hills here and there. A bit farther, things can become quite muddy as the trail passes through a low-lying marshy area. During my visit, the trail was very wet and sloppy in this area but much better just beyond it. As you continue toward the falls, you'll eventually start to follow the Carp River upstream. There are some pretty spots along the way, as the river winds and cascades over the rocky riverbed. When you reach the falls, a convenient bench awaits, making it easy to relax and enjoy this cascading falls.

Overlooked Falls

Greenstone Falls

Overlooked Falls & Greenstone Falls

LOCATION: Porcupine Mountains Wilderness State Park

ADDRESS/GPS FOR THE FALLS: Overlooked Falls: 46° 43.214′ N, 89° 49.547′ W; Greenstone Falls: 46° 43.436′ N, 89° 49.904′ W

DIRECTIONS: Starting at the Presque Isle River area on the western side of the Porcupine Mountains, drive east on S. Boundary Rd. After 8 miles, turn left onto Little Carp River Rd. Follow for 0.2 mile, then turn right at the gate, into the parking area. (A pit toilet is available here.)

WEBSITE: www.michigandnr.com/parksandtrails/Details.aspx?type=SPRK&id=426

WATERWAY: Little Carp River

HEIGHT: Overlooked Falls: 8 feet; Greenstone Falls: 6 feet **CREST:** Overlooked Falls: 40 feet; Greenstone Falls: 25 feet

NEAREST TOWN: Wakefield

HIKE DIFFICULTY: Overlooked Falls: Easy; Greenstone Falls: Fair, small hills and narrow wood planks

TRAIL QUALITY: Overlooked Falls: Good, dirt road and narrow trail; Greenstone Falls: Good, narrow trail

ROUND-TRIP DISTANCE: Overlooked Falls: 0.8 mile; Greenstone Falls: 1.8 miles

ADMISSION: Michigan Recreation Passport required (see page 12)

TRIP REPORT & TIPS:

Located in the southwest corner of the park, both of these falls are relatively close to each other on the Little Carp River. They aren't the biggest or best in the park, but they're definitely worth a visit if you have the time.

Between the two, I prefer Overlooked Falls because of its character and wild look. Greenstone Falls is very uniform and symmetrical, with little to no flare. To see both, walk past the gate and follow the dirt road down the hill. Just before the wide footbridge across the river, there's a narrow trail marked with a sign for Overlooked Falls. The trail heads left into the woods. Follow for 250 feet to the falls. For Greenstone Falls, walk over the wide footbridge and head to the left on the Little Carp River Trail. Follow this trail along the river for 0.5 mile. A sign marks where the falls is located. To see the falls at the base, you need to climb down the bank to get a view from the river's edge.

Shining Cloud Falls

LOCATION: Porcupine Mountains Wilderness State Park

ADDRESS/GPS FOR THE FALLS: 46° 45.466' N, 89° 51.987' W

DIRECTIONS: Starting at the Presque Isle River area on the western side of the Porkies, drive east on S. Boundary Rd. After 4.4 miles, turn left into the roadside parking lot for the Pinkerton Trailhead. (The lot also has a pit toilet.)

WEBSITE: www.michigandnr.com/parksandtrails/Details.aspx?type=SPRK&id=426

WATERWAY: Big Carp River

HEIGHT: 36 feet **CREST:** 54 feet

NEAREST TOWN: Wakefield

HIKE DIFFICULTY: Difficult

TRAIL QUALITY: Fair

ROUND-TRIP DISTANCE: 10.6 miles

ADMISSION: Michigan Recreation Passport required (see page 12)

TRIP REPORT & TIPS:

Shining Cloud Falls lives up to its name, as it's shining gem of a waterfall in a remote part of the park. The hike to the falls is just as rewarding as the cataract itself. On the route described here, you'll travel through some incredible forest with towering trees, hike a ridgeline with scenic views, travel along the Lake Superior shoreline, and follow the beautiful, crystal-clear Big Carp River upstream.

Similar to the other remote waterfalls in the Porcupine Mountains, there are a few different trails and routes you can take. I chose the shortest route there; it starts with the Pinkerton Trail (2.4 miles), then connects to the Lake Superior Trail (1.5 miles) and finally the Big Carp River Trail (1.4 miles).

As you can tell by the distance, this is a long hike, so be sure to bring plenty of food and water. The terrain is generally hilly, but there are a few steeper sections, too. When you do finally come to the falls, the view from the trail is not great, as the falls are down in a deep gorge. For the optimum view, you'll first want to climb down the hillside before the top of the falls and then work your way back downstream. To get to the base, I ended up walking down the side of the falls on the sloping rock next to the gorge wall. Fortunately, it was dry, so the footing was good. Once at the base, you get a great view of this divided waterfall and the calm, rocky pool at the base.

Nonesuch Falls

LOCATION: Porcupine Mountains Wilderness State Park

ADDRESS/GPS FOR THE FALLS: 46° 45.207' N, 89° 37.199' W

DIRECTIONS: From the Porcupine Mountains Visitor Center turn right (south) on South Boundary Rd. Drive for 3.8 miles. You'll see an unmarked dirt road veer to the left as the main paved road bends to the right. Turn onto this dirt road, and drive a short distance to the parking area. Information signs will note that you're near the Nonesuch Mine.

WEBSITE: www.michigandnr.com/parksandtrails/Details.aspx?type=SPRK&id=426

WATERWAY: Little Iron River

HEIGHT: 13 feet **CREST:** 45 feet

NEAREST TOWN: Silver City

HIKE DIFFICULTY: Fair

TRAIL QUALITY: Good, with some small hills and tree roots

ROUND-TRIP DISTANCE: 1 mile

ADMISSION: No fee

TRIP REPORT & TIPS:

Nonesuch Falls is best viewed during the wetter seasons, as it can dry up in July and August. The area near the falls is interesting. The Nonesuch Copper Mine once operated here; today, the remains from this mine are visible, with large stone foundations as well as some equipment.

After parking, walk around the gate and follow the grassy two-track trail, which will lead into the woods. To your left, you'll see narrower trails heading downhill. Follow these trails to see the mining ruins, as well as the waterfall when you reach the river.

21 More Waterfalls to Explore

	GPS Coordinates	Location	Height
	Whitefish Falls 46° 13.066' N 87° 03.003' W	Trenary	5 feet and 2.5 feet
	Rapid River Falls 46° 01.313' N 86° 58.914' W	Rapid River Falls Park.	4 feet
	Haymeadow Falls 46° 01.550' N 86° 51.235' W	Hiawatha National Forest	3 feet
	Silver Falls (Silver Bell Falls) 46° 27.064' N 86° 58.248' W	Rock River Canyon Wilderness, Hiawatha National Forest	20 feet
	Potato Patch Falls 46° 29.921' N 86° 31.815' W	Pictured Rocks National Lakeshore	36 feet
	Ely Falls 46° 26.312' N 87° 41.212' W	Southwest of Ishpeming	5 feet

	GPS Coordinates	Location	Height
	Nelligan Creek Falls 46° 33.083' N 88° 08.068' W	Craig Lake State Park	5 feet
	Reany Falls 46° 34.410' N 87° 28.614' W	Near Marquette	11 feet (several small drops)
	Midway Creek Falls Falls 1: 46° 33.121' N 87° 29.859' W; Falls 2: 46° 33.140' N 87° 29.867' W	Vielmetti-Peters Conservation Reserve	Falls 1 (two-levels): 14 feet; Falls 2: 6 feet
	Erick's Falls 46° 48.395' N 88° 05.225' W	Skanee	6 feet
	Ravine River Road Falls 46° 46.519' N 88° 09.991' W	En route to Mt. Arvon	7 feet
	Tioga River – Unnamed 46° 34.407' N 88° 20.377' W	Roadside Rest Area east of Covington	6 feet

21 More Waterfalls to Explore

	GPS Coordinates	Location	Height
	Tibbets Falls 46° 34.899' N 88° 35.357' W	Northwest of Covington	15 feet (long stair-step cascade)
	Page Creek Falls 46° 45.456' N 88° 21.398' W	A side creek near Middle Silver Falls	8 feet
	Redridge Falls Dam 47° 08.911' N 88° 45.867' W	West of Houghton	Steel dam: 67 feet; log crib dam: 16 feet
	Conglomerate Falls (Upper Gratiot River Falls) 47° 19.833' N 88° 26.045' W	3 miles northwest of Ahmeek	16 feet (long, gradual slide)
	Eister Falls 47° 22.009' N 88° 07.981' W	Near Phoenix, Michigan Nature Association	17 feet (3 cascades)
	Tobacco River Falls 47° 13.876' N 88° 08.926' W	1 mile northeast of Gay	5 feet

	GPS Coordinates	Location	Height
	Horse Race Rapids 45° 59.410' N 88° 16.147' W	Close to Michigan/ Wisconsin border	Rapids
	Wright Street Falls 46° 33.938' N 87° 26.728' W	City of Marquette	11 feet
	Trapper's Falls 46° 44.004' N 89° 53.125' W	Porcupine Mountains, northwest of Greenstone Falls	24 feet

Michigan Waterfalls Checklist

Western U.P.

Keweenaw Peninsula

Black River Scenic Byway/The Porcupine Mountains

About the Author

Greg Kretovic is a proud Yooper who lives in the beautiful Upper Peninsula of Michigan. Since moving to the U.P. to attend Northern Michigan University, where he earned a BFA in Art and Design, he has enjoyed living in this special part of the state as well as seeing and doing all that the area has to offer. Along the way, he started photographing the landscapes, waterfalls, seasons and more. Greg is also known for his photographs of the mighty Lake Superior—the greatest of the Great Lakes. He has sold prints throughout the U.S. and has had his work published in magazines, television, news media and advertising. When Greg isn't out photographing he works as a freelance graphic/web designer. He also enjoys a variety of outdoor activities including cross-country skiing, running, fishing, hiking and camping with his family.

To view more of Greg's photography or to order prints of the waterfalls in this book, visit his website www.MichiganNaturePhotos.com. He is also active on social media so search for him on there, as well.